WHAT'S THE DIFFERENCE?

A *cover-up* is simply an effort to prevent investigation or exposure of action. That can include—but is not limited to—doctoring documents, destroying evidence, and bribery.

A *whitewash* is the use of words or actions in an effort to absolve a person or group from blame in a criminal act, scandal, etc. In other words, it's a lie.

A *will* is the legal statement of a person's wishes regarding the disposal of his or her estate and of other matters to be performed after death.

A *testament* is the section of a will that relates solely to the disposition of property.

**To discover the vital differences
between many other words, read on!**

Also by Jeff Rovin
Published by Ballantine Books:

LAWS OF ORDER
A Book of Hierarchies, Rankings, Infrastructures, Measurements, and Sizes

WHAT'S THE DIFFERENCE?

A Compendium of Commonly
Confused and Misused Words

Jeff Rovin

BALLANTINE BOOKS • NEW YORK

Copyright © 1994 by Jeff Rovin

All rights reserved under International and Pan-American Copyright Conventions. Published in the United States of America by Ballantine Books, a division of Random House, Inc., New York, and simultaneously in Canada by Random House of Canada Limited, Toronto.

Library of Congress Catalog Card Number: 94-94416

ISBN 0-345-37827-X

Manufactured in the United States of America

First Edition: December 1994

10 9 8 7 6 5 4 3 2 1

TABLE OF CONTENTS

Is this an ...

Introduction, Foreword, or Preface?

Let's be up-front about this: there's more than one way to start a book.

Like this one, for example. Since the author is writing the section, it can't be a *foreword*. That's always penned by someone else, and its purpose is to recommend the author, the book, or (hopefully) both.

Are you reading an *introduction*, then? No, because while those are written by the author, they go into quite a bit of detail regarding the creation of the book and why it's needed. They also present an overview of the subject.

No, this is a *preface*, a brief chapter that says "hi," tells you the reason the book was written (the words in this volume are pesky, and dictionary definitions are frustratingly terse), explains how the subject was researched (in *The Oxford English Dictionary* and in texts devoted to the words and topics in question; see *Selected Bibliography*), and thanks those whose input was invaluable (editor Elizabeth Zack and consultants Dr. Kenneth Ogan, Dr. Orlito Trias, J. Q. LaFond of the Connecticut Conservatory, and many others).

So before this becomes a long-winded introduction—enjoy!

THE HUMAN BODY

Persons/People

Go to any ritzy restaurant and the hostess will probably ask you, "How many persons are in your party?"

Why isn't it, "How many people are in your party?" Because you're in a fancy place, and you're being accorded a measure of respect.

People is a term equivalent to "cows" and "horses": it's "a herd" of us humans. People is a word that simply distinguishes us from the other animals out there.

Persons, on the other hand, signifies people in terms of our external aspects: our bodies, our features, and even our clothing. In other words, the individuals as opposed to the masses.

(Obviously, that magazine about the cavalcade of humankind was correctly named.)

Dwarf/Midget/Pygmy

Author Jonathan Swift had a low opinion of both people *and* persons. As he pointed out metaphorically in *Gulliver's Travels*, the tiny Lilliputians and the giant Brobdingnagians were equally petty and vindictive.

Swift was an incurable cynic, but he was correct about one thing: people *are* the same, regardless of their shape or size. Here is how some of our smaller people are classified.

A *dwarf* is a person who is smaller than average in size and who is not proportioned the same as a person of average height.

A *midget* is a small person who's otherwise proportioned

2

the same as a full-grown individual. Typically, an adult midget is between four feet and four foot eight.

A *pygmy* is two things. Anthropologically, it's a member ⬛ny number of races of correctly proportioned people of ⬛ry small stature found in Equatorial Africa, the Philippines, and Southeast Asia. In general usage, however, it's a perfectly proportioned human who is smaller than a midget.

Cranium/Skull

At some point in the development of slang, "bonehead" came to be synonymous with the concept of "dunce." The implication, of course, is that the individual's head is solid bone. But the truth is, without a bony head, human life would be impossible.

The *skull* is the bony framework of the head, consisting of thirteen separate bones that enclose the brain and support the flesh, scalp, and elements of the face.

The *cranium* is the part of the skull that encloses the brain; it consists of all the bones of the skull except for one, the inferior maxillary or mandible (the lower jaw).

Artery/Capillary/Vein

Here are some facts that every red-blooded American should know about the circulatory system.

There are seventy thousand miles of blood vessels in the average adult body; incredibly, the heart pumps blood through the network once a minute.

This remarkable circulatory system consists of three kinds of vessels:

An *artery*, any one of the many tubes that carry clean, oxygenated blood from the heart to all parts of the body.

A *vein*, any of the canals that return impure blood from the organs and tissues back to the heart.

A *capillary*, a very small blood vessel whose branchlike masses connect the ends of arteries to the beginnings of veins so that blood can circulate throughout the body.

Ligament/Tendon

Like capillaries, connective matter is as important to the body as organs, muscles, and bones. Take ligaments tendons, for example.

Ligaments are the tough connective material that hold bones together. *Tendons* are the fibrous section of muscles that attach them to bones; the term *sinew* is synonymous with tendon.

Both are forms of soft tissue, a substance that is much tougher than its reputation gives it credit for. Read on for more on the subject.

Membrane/Tissue

A *tissue* is a collection of cells that form a thin but tough structural material in plants or animals. Each kind of tissue has a specific function, such as cicatricial (scar) tissue; connective tissue such as cartilage; fibrous tissue (ligaments, tendons [see entry, above]); and parenchymatous tissue, of which the organs are made.

A *membrane* is a very thin, pliable layer of animal or vegetable tissue. Its different types include fetal tissue, which surrounds the embryo inside the uterus; mucous tissue, which lines the throat, nose, and organs such as the lungs and intestines; the tympanic membrane, which forms the eardrum; and many others.

Obviously, "tissue" wasn't the most accurate word Scott, Kleenex, et al., could have chosen for their product, but "two-ply membranes" has a rather ghastly ring to it. Sometimes, propriety must come before accuracy! . . .

Nude/Naked

Moving to the outside of the body, the distinction between being *naked* and being *nude* is barely made anymore (so to speak); for all practical purposes, the words are interchangeable. But if you want to get nit-picky about it, there's a reason the folks are called "nudists" and not "nakedists," and why truth is naked but not nude.

Both words come from the Latin *nudus*, though *naked* took a detour through Old English *(nacod)* to take on its slightly different meaning.

One who is *naked* is totally bare, *in puris naturalibus*, wearing nothing but an expression. One who is *nude* has become that way by *removing* their clothes. A newborn baby, for example, is naked but not nude—until its first diaper comes off. A jaybird (a rural youth, not one of our feathered friends) is naked because he/she never bothers to dress. And truth is naked because, according to legend, truth and falsehood were bathing when falsehood suddenly bolted from the stream, donned truth's clothes, and ran off. Rather than wear the cloak of falsehood, truth remained naked.

And those are the raw facts.

Midriff/Waist

While we're still unclothed, let's have a look down and face the bad news for dieters who thought that a thickening waist and a bulging midriff were one and the same: nope. They're two separate problems.

The *waist* lies above the hips and below the lowest ribs and circles the entire body. The *midriff* is the section of the human body that reaches from just above the waist up to the bottom of the sternum and reaches around the sides to (but does not include) the back.

The slang term "spare tire" refers to a fat waist, while a "beer belly" is a midriff that protrudes in the front; both terms have been in use since the early 1920s.

Now, moving further south . . .

Crotch/Groin/Loins

The *crotch* is the area formed by the joining of the two legs or limbs, on the human body (or on a pair of pants), on an animal, or in a tree.

The *groin* is the depression or hollow of the body where the abdomen meets each hip.

The *loins* are the parts of the body of a human or other

quadruped or biped located between the lowest ribs and the hip bone, both front and back.

Of the three, loins is the only term that includes the reproductive organs, which is why they're regarded as the seat of generative power. Despite that fact, the other two words have become synonymous with the genitalia. Linguists suggest that because loins was used in both the Bible and literature, crotch and groin took their secondary meaning sometime in the eighteenth century to suggest intentions that were anything but lofty or poetic.

It may seem a little odd to picture people in powdered wigs using words like these, though these *are* the same people whose men wore codpieces to enhance the appearance of masculinity, and who gave the name of a noted Civil War general to women who practiced the world's oldest profession. . . .

Burnsides/Muttonchops/Sideburns

The Union's Gen. Joseph Hooker wasn't the only Civil War officer whose name became part of the language, although he probably would have preferred to be remembered for something other than the ladies of the night in whose company his men were regularly seen. How he must have envied fellow officer, Gen. Ambrose Burnside, who is remembered for the distinctive set of whiskers he wore: a mustache and full beard, except on the chin, which was clean-shaven. Today, these kinds of whiskers are called *burnsides*.

The variation *sideburns* was coined to describe those whiskers worn only on the side of the face—generally from the hairline to no lower than the bottom of the ear.

Muttonchops are long sideburns that reach down to the jawline and forward to the chin, although both of these areas remain clean-shaven. These whiskers have a somewhat less distinguished etymology than the others, as they take their name from their resemblance to a mutton or lambchop—which no one would consider a fashion statement!

THE HUMAN MIND

Egocentricity/Egoism/Egotism

There's an old joke about an egotist who corners someone at a party. After talking for quite some time, the egotist says, "But enough about *me*. What do *you* think of me?"

According to Freud, the ego (from the Latin for "I") is one of the three components of human psychic makeup, the others being the id (primitive instinct) and the superego (conscience). Many of us know people for whom the ego constitutes ninety percent or more of their psychic makeup; unfortunately, Freud made no guarantees about proportions.

The ego is that which looks after and promotes the self by balancing the demands of the id with those of the superego. There are dozens of subdivisions of the ego: ego-object polarity, ego-dystonic homosexuality, and the like. But the most commonly encountered forms are the following:

Egocentricity, which is total self-absorption, manifested not just in preoccupation with the self but in insensitivity to others. (It stops short, however, of malicious *egopathy*, which is the bolstering of the self by the knocking down of others.)

Egoism, which doesn't exclude sensitivity to others, but allows it if—and only if—self-interest has first been served and completely satisfied.

Egotism, which is not self-interest per se, but a wild overestimation of one's own importance, talents, opinions, etc. In other words, the bore at a cocktail party is an *egotist*.

Anxious/Nervous

What, me worry?

Sure, we all do. But being worried about something that's happening now and something that's going to happen in the future are two very different things.

If you're highly excitable, on edge, and agitated because of something that's going on now, usually within the range of sight or hearing, then you're *nervous*.

If you're full of distress and uneasiness due to possible danger or misfortune in the future or outside your immediate area, then you're *anxious*. You can be anxious about bee stings when you go outside during the summer, or about bumping into a ghost at midnight, but you can only be nervous as you tiptoe past a beehive, through a graveyard, etc.

Unfortunately, there's something even worse you might experience as you do either of these two things. . . .

Horror/Terror

Movies about swarms of killer bees or ghosts are called "horror movies." So why are so many of them advertised with lines like, "It will fill you with terror!"? And why does a terrorist leave behind a scene of horror?

Because sometimes, horror just isn't strong enough, or terror is too quick.

Horror is an emotion comprised of fear, dread, and abhorrence—a feeling aroused by something frightful and shocking.

Terror arouses the same feelings, only much more intensely, and usually for a shorter period of time. The line, "It will fill you with terror!" is implying that the movie will shock you over and over and over again.

Also, horror is typically used to describe the tone of an entire situation or piece, whereas terror is attached to specific moments. For example, *The Exorcist* is a horror film, but young Regan turning her head entirely around is intended to inspire terror.

Effeminate/Feminine

Here's a pair of words that no one would ever apply to little Regan MacNeil.

Although society is moving in fits and starts toward greater equality between the sexes, biology is not—and happily so. So there are aspects of our species (indeed, of all species) that are inherently male and female.

Feminine describes any characteristic, physical trait, look, habit, or biological process that belongs to the female sex or pertains to females. The word applies to any species, though what is feminine for lions, for example—hunting and gutting prey—may not necessarily apply to other females, such as humans.

Conversely, effeminacy is not for women but for men. *Effeminate* describes any traditionally female traits, such as softness and delicacy, when they appear in a human male.

Scientists no longer believe that effeminacy is caused by environment but by the fact that a certain part of the brain of some men is larger than that of other men. Scientists don't know why this is true, only that autopsies confirm it. But there's a lot science doesn't know—for instance . . .

Hypnotism/Mesmerism

Scientists do not know why some people are more easily hypnotized than others. The process can take seconds or hours, and many people do not respond to it as deeply as others. Some don't even respond to it at all!

Hypnotism is the use of gentle, rhythmic stimuli, such as the quiet voice of the hypnotist or a soft, pulsing light, to induce a state that resembles sleep but isn't, a state characterized by heightened susceptibility to suggestion. Many subjects who have been hypnotized can be cured of habits, made to comprehend or retain information, regressed to childhood (or previous lives, as some hypnotists claim), and so forth.

Mesmerism is simply a powerful state of hypnosis practiced by F. A. Mesmer, an eighteenth-century Austrian physician. Mesmer insisted that he was a conduit for a magnetic power that pervaded the universe; although that seems a rather egotistical claim, reportedly he was able to mesmerize patients with a long, intense glance or with very few commands, and cure them of many ailments.

Clairvoyance/ESP/Precognition/Telepathy

Mesmerism is an impressive feat, but there are other powers that cross the line into the realm of the incredible. Studies at Duke University and elsewhere suggest that these powers exist, but, once more, scientists and parapsychologists are unable to fully fathom or explain them.

ESP—extrasensory perception—is any communication with and/or awareness of objects or people beyond the reach of the five senses.

Clairvoyance is a particular kind of ESP, the ability to see things or activity beyond the range of normal vision.

Telepathy is a different form of ESP, nonverbal communication from one mind directly to another, usually over a considerable distance.

Precognition is a third type of ESP, an awareness of the shape that events will take before they occur. Precognition reportedly comes to some people in the form of dreams, trances, or as a visual experience—for example, seeing a black shadow or "death aura" around one who is soon to die.

For those who want to try and avoid nasty umbrae like that, have a look at . . .

HEALTH

Ophthalmologist/Optometrist/Optician

In his or her own way, each of these professionals is a sight for sore eyes.

An *ophthalmologist* is a doctor who can treat the eye medically or surgically. An *optometrist* is also a doctor, but one who is only permitted to examine the eyes and prescribe glasses, or, in certain cases, eyedrops. An *optician* makes glasses, period.

See the difference?

In case you're wondering, the first, oft-forgotten "h" in ophthalmologist is due to the fact that that word has a different root than the others: the Greek *ophthalmos* for "eye," as opposed to *optos* for "seen."

Plaque/Tartar

Here's a distinction you can really sink your teeth into.

If your pearly whites are covered with a gelatinous film containing saliva and bacteria, it's *plaque*. If the plaque is allowed to collect it forms *tartar*, *aka* dental calculus, a harder, brownish yellow deposit also comprised of food particles and salts such as phosphate and calcium carbonate.

So make sure you clean your teeth regularly with a dentifrice (a blanket term for toothpastes), or a cleansing powder.

Boil/Bunion/Corn/Carbuncle

Here's a burning question: Why do aching bunions allow some people to predict a coming rainstorm? Why not throbbing corns or carbuncles?

Because a *bunion* is an inflammation and swelling of the bursa (a sac at the joint) at the base of the big toe. Joints swell or contract by absorbing moisture, thus making bunions reliable barometers.

Conversely, a *corn* is a horny thickening of the skin, caused by friction or compression. It's usually painful when touched, and can be located anywhere on the body, but generally found on the feet and/or toes. (People who *think* their corns are forecasting the weather don't really have corns but bunions.)

A *boil* (*aka* a *furuncle*) is an inflamed, pus-filled swelling on the skin that is caused by an infection. A *carbuncle* is a larger and more serious pus-filled inflammation of the underlying tissue.

Yum.

Diagnosis/Prognosis

You're sick. Not with aching corns, but with something more serious.

You hate going to the doctor, but, ill with abdominal cramps, a slight fever, and nausea, you reluctantly leave your office and go to hers. After examining you and confirming that you're a wreck, the M.D. asks what you had for lunch. When you tell her, she nods. Your ailments, plus the fact that you ate several orders of sushi, suggest trichinosis. That conclusion is her *diagnosis*.

The doctor prescribes *Colocynthis* and *Cuprum arsenicosum*; if you take them once every two hours, she feels confident that you'll recover. That prediction is her *prognosis*.

(And the moral of the story is, always go to doctors to find out what they nosis.)

Clinic/Dispensary/Hospital/Infirmary

If you don't have medical insurance, you'll be getting your diagnosis in a *dispensary*, a charitable institution where medicines and, often, medical care are given free to those in need. If you're "covered," your options for care are greater. Available to you are:

A *hospital*, an institution where the ill or debilitated can receive medical attention, surgery, physical therapy, and even psychiatric care; and a *clinic*, which is usually affiliated with a hospital or medical school. It's a place where patients from the world over can come to be treated by specialists in various areas who practice as a group.

For company employees—especially those of union establishments—there's also an *infirmary*, a room or section of a building that serves as a small hospital and is usually staffed by a nurse.

Bacterium/Microbe/Virus

As you lie there in bed, sick as can be, you begin to wonder just what *causes* trichinosis. You discover it's a worm called *Trichinella spiralis*, which is disgusting; you were expecting a microbe of some kind, something small and invisible. (Worms are *parasites*, organisms that live off a host, only occasionally causing their death.)

A *microbe* (or *germ*) is a microorganism that can be parasitic, though the term microbe usually applies to *bacterium*. A bacterium (bacteria if there's more than one, which there always is when you're ill) is any of the microscopic, usually single-celled organisms shaped like spheres, rods, or spirals, which are involved not only in causing disease, but putrefaction, fermentation, and other activities.

A *virus* is smaller still and often more nefarious in its activities (virus and virulent share the same Latin root, *vīru*, for "poison"). It's an ultramicroscopic infectious agent that invades and reproduces only in living cells. Outside the cells, they seem completely lifeless.

Graft/Splice

If illness or an accident gets the best of you, there's a possibility you'll be hearing about one of these.

To *graft* is to take a section of one thing and make it adhere to and become part of another by insertion or implantation, such as a skin graft or a plant graft (where a shoot of one plant is placed in a slit in the stem of another so that it will grow). Grafting is a common medical practice, particularly for burn victims, though the use of fetal tissue for grafting remains controversial.

To *splice* is to join two objects end to end to make them whole. It may be two parts of what was once a single object, such as a broken bone, or it may be two previously unrelated elements, such as different genes—a subject also very much in the news, since mutant genes are the result—or scenes in a motion picture.

Naturally, it had to be graft, not splice, that was used to signify a form of corruption: the goal of graft is to make what was stolen appear to be a natural part of a whole, rather than something that was tacked on.

Pellet/Pill/Tablet

Defeat may be a bitter pill for some to swallow, but imagine how tough it would be to gulp down a tablet of defeat. On the other hand, a pellet of defeat wouldn't be nearly as bad.

Pellet comes from the Latin *pila*, or "ball," and is a small, spherical form of medicine meant to be dissolved in liquid or ground up and mixed with other substances. Today, the word is used primarily for animal medicines *or* to describe the tiny medicinal balls contained in capsules.

Pill derives from the same Latin root and describes a flattened, round, or oval mass. Pills are small and are designed to be swallowed whole.

Tablet, from the Latin *tabula*, or "board," describes any substance pressed into a flat, usually elongated oval that's larger than a pill. Today, the word is primarily used in connection with medicine, though it can also be applied to cubes of sugar, bouillon, etc. (And the truth is, sometimes a bouillon cube will work just as well as many medicine tablets.)

Isolation/Quarantine

In the days before trains and planes, when goods were transported by sea, ships on which a communicable disease had broken out were kept in port or at sea for forty days—a time period that allowed most diseases to run their course and/or kill the crew. The Italians called this period *quarantina*—"forty days"—which was anglicized as *quarantine*.

The difference between this kind of segregation and *isolation* is that the latter was imposed not on those who had the disease, but on those who had been exposed to it, typically in another port of call. If, in isolation, the crew showed no signs of coming down with the illness, they were then allowed to dock. If anyone became sick, the entire crew was usually quarantined.

In recent decades, however, both procedures have become less necessary thanks to inoculations. Or is that vaccinations?

Immunization/Inoculation/Vaccination

The body responds to disease by sending antibodies to attack the responsible agent. If the body was exposed to the agent previously, defense is that much easier. Thus, weakened or dead forms of the disease are administered to children, allowing their bodies to build up defenses in case the real McCoy ever rears its head.

The term vaccine originally applied only to the modified smallpox virus—*aka* cowpox (*vacca* is Latin for "cow")—developed by Dr. Edward Jenner in the late eighteenth century, which was used to build an immunity to that disease. It was administered by *vaccination*, scratching the skin with a needle that had been dipped in virus-infected serum.

Later, the term vaccine was applied to other serums, such as the Salk polio vaccine, which were not given via pricking the skin but by hypodermic needle. Hence, *vaccination* was replaced by *inoculation*, which described any method of preventative medicine involving a poke, scratch, or injection.

Still, that didn't cover Sabin's oral polio vaccine or various suppositories, implants, and such. Thus, nowadays, the blanket term *immunization* is used, which pretty much says it all.

Carcinoma/Melanoma/Sarcoma

Cancer is a word that describes any malignant and invasive growth. Like the Hydra of mythology, it's a killer with many faces, each with its own awful expression. Three of these faces, which are often confused, are the following.

Carcinoma is a malignant tumor of cells that line the organs. Not only does it affect the organs, but it can spread elsewhere through the bloodstream; often, because it can migrate and take root elsewhere, it will recur even after excision.

Melanoma is a cancer that grows from those cells containing pigment—for example, a mole.

Sarcoma is a cancer that begins in bone or in connective tissue and spreads among bone, muscle, cartilage, fat, etc.

When detected early enough, many forms of cancer can be treated by surgical removal, radiation therapy, or chemotherapy—the use of toxic chemicals. Killing cancer is not always the problem, per se; the trick is killing it without damaging the healthy cells around it.

Cadaver/Carcass/Corpse/Remains

When the body dies, it becomes at least two—and possibly three—things, depending on what is done with it.

A *corpse* is the dead body of a human being that is still relatively intact and has not been embalmed.

A *cadaver* is the dead body of a human being that has undergone dissection—hopefully by a coroner or medical students!

If a body is embalmed, if major sections have been removed in dissection or as a result of an accident, or if a good deal of the soft tissue has fallen away over time, what's left are *remains*.

The term *carcass* is generally used to describe slaughtered animals from which the inedible sections have been removed—though the term can also be applied disparagingly to humans.

RELIGION

Atheism/Agnosticism/Pantheism

When medical science fails, many people turn to religion for comfort, although that's not an option for those who disavow a supreme being or question God's existence.

Atheism is a complete disbelief in God. There's no afterlife, no moral arbiter, no creator other than the blind forces of nature.

Agnosticism is a more temperate point of view: it does not profess to know whether there is or isn't a God, but maintains that, in any case, it's impossible to know. Most agnostics believe that only when we die will we know for sure.

Pantheism advocates the idea that God is not a being per se, but that all the matter, forces, and laws of the universe—in short, all of nature—are manifestations of God.

Historically, nonbelievers clash with those who worship a god of some kind. That's understandable; by their very existence, one group is tacitly calling the other group ignorant. What's less comprehensible is how the God-fearing describe other believers as nonbelievers simply because they worship a different god or gods, to wit . . .

Heathen/Infidel/Pagan

A *heathen* (from the Gothic for "wasteland dweller") was originally any polytheist, such as a member of the idol-worshiping faiths of ancient Egypt, Greece, Rome, etc. During the Crusades, however, the term came to mean anyone who did not acknowledge the one true God—which, naturally, made one person's heathen another person's saint. To Moslems, followers of Judeo-Christian religions were (and are) heathens, and vice versa.

Infidel, from the Latin *infidelus*, for "unfaithful," is a heathen who doesn't believe in the prevailing religion of the land. Christians who were living in Moslem-dominated countries during the Crusades were branded as heathens and infidels; to those Christians, the Moslems were simply heathens.

A *pagan* is a heathen who worships earth gods through roots, stones, water, and so forth. (The term itself comes from the Latin *pagus*, for "country.") The druids of the ancient Celts and Gauls, for example, were priests of various pagan faiths. Contrary to popular belief, pagan religions have not died out; they are practiced worldwide just as they were in the past: in small, private groups.

Middle Ages/Dark Ages

The rise of Christianity helped bring about the disintegration of the Roman Empire, which accelerated during the short reign of the last Roman emperor, Romulus (A.D. 465–66). His brief tenure not only signified the end of an empire but the loss of the primary civilizing force in the world. As a result, the world slipped into *The Dark Ages*, a period of some five hundred years when research, culture, and teaching came to a virtual standstill, and deplorable living conditions were rampant throughout Europe and parts of Asia and the Middle East.

Spurred by more enlightened rulers, civilization began to make a comeback, of sorts, around A.D. 1000, a progress that built slowly to the Renaissance, which lasted from the fourteenth to the seventeenth centuries. *The Middle Ages* (or *Medieval Age*) comprises the entire period between the fall of Rome and the emergence of the Renaissance, and is broken into the *early Middle Ages* (concurrent with the Dark Ages), the High Middle Ages (circa 1000–1300) and the late Middle Ages (1300–the Renaissance). The Renaissance was, of course, a time of the great revival of art, literature, and learning in Europe.

Hades/Hell

As far as most devoutly religious people are concerned, all atheists, heathens, infidels, and pagans are damned and headed for a most unpleasant afterlife.

However, the underworld has undergone some changes since the Greek poet Orpheus went below to convince the god Hades and Queen Persephone to release his dead bride Eurydice.

In Greek mythology, *Hades*—the name of both the god and the place—is a carefully delineated realm to which all souls, those good and bad, go upon death. The ferrryman Charon escorts the dead across the river Styx, one of the five rivers that surround the underworld; there, souls enter the gates of Hades, which are guarded by the three-headed dog Cerberus, who allows souls to enter but not to leave. Beyond these gates, Hades is divided into three sections: Erebus, to which all of the dead go immediately upon dying; Tartarus, the deeper part in which the sinners are punished; and the Elysian Fields, a place of beauty in which the just spend eternity.

Hell was created using elements taken from Hades and the Norse Niflheim, which was the underworld ruled by Hel, the evil goddess of the dead. In Judeo-Christian teachings, hell is a realm ruled by the fallen angel Satan, a place of fire and torment where the souls of evildoers, the unbaptized, etc., are damned for eternity by being tortured by various devils and demons.

Poets such as Dante, in *The Divine Comedy*, and John Milton, in *Paradise Lost*, have elaborated upon religious writings and have described hell in great detail. Hopefully, we'll never know if they're right or wrong.

Demon/Devil

Religion and literature agree on one topic. There are two kinds of denizens serving Satan: devils and demons, creatures with certain similarities and a few distinct differences.

Devils—of which Satan is the chief one, often called the Devil—are evil beings who carry out Satan's wishes in hell. Devils are typically portrayed as having horns, cloven hooves, a tail, and red flesh; they're said to be angels that fell from heaven with Satan.

Demons are regarded as the spirits of the damned who are sent to work evil in our world. They're often attached to specific places, such as wells, caves, or woods, and their task is to woo people to wickedness by haunting their dreams, possessing their bodies, offering them riches for their souls, etc., and thus creating more demons.

Some Middle Eastern sects regard genies (*aka* djinnis or djinns) as demons, as they grant us our fondest wishes in order to corrupt us and increase the genie-pool.

Apostle/Disciple

On the opposite end of the spectrum from those who serve the devil are those who serve as holy men—the apostles and disciples.

Disciple comes from the Latin *discipulus* ("pupil") and was originally used to describe any of the followers of Jesus during his lifetime. Afterward, it came to mean anyone who was an adherent or pupil of another who taught religion, philosophy, or some branch of science, medicine, or psychology, typically in a new or controversial way.

An *apostle*, from the Greek *apostolos* ("one who is sent out"), originally applied to one of the twelve disciples sent forth by Jesus to preach the gospel. Unlike disciple, it hasn't taken on any significant other meaning. (And despite the pronunciation of Orson Welles and many other rhetors, the "t" is silent.)

Chapel/Church

Lerner and Loewe wrote a memorable tune for *My Fair Lady* about getting Eliza Doolittle to the church on time to marry. Meanwhile, over on the pop charts, The Dixie Cups sang about tying the knot in the "Chapel of Love."

Is there any chance it could have been a double wedding? Unlikely.

A *church* is a building for public Christian worship and ceremonies. A *chapel* is a small place of prayer, worship, or ceremony for Christians. It may be a separate part of a church, a distinct building, or a private room in some other institution.

A chapel wedding suggests a small and private affair. A wedding in "the chapel of love" suggests something tackier—not a place in which Eliza's love, Professor Higgins, would be caught dead, let alone wed!

Spire/Steeple

Back in the old days, when horses raced through courses with hedges, ditches, and fences, the rider kept the horse on track by looking for the highest object around: the local church steeple. Thus, the races came to be known as steeplechases.

But what, exactly, was the rider looking at? Should the old races more correctly have been called *spire*chases?

Steeples are ornamental constructions of various shapes and sizes that sit on the roof of a house of worship or public building. The lower portion of the steeple is often a *cupola*, a structure that may be decorative, or may serve as a belfry or belvedere, while the upper, pointed portion, is the *spire*.

So, chances are good the steeplechase riders weren't looking at steeples but at something else. You might say their riding was more in*spired*.

Canticle/Hymn/Litany/Psalm

Prayer was probably invented by the first spearless cave person who was cornered by a saber-toothed tiger. Since that time, communication with God and other deities, or celebrations of them, have taken many ritualized forms. In addition to prayer, which is defined as a devout petition to or spiritual communication with God, there are:

A *hymn*, a song or ode praising or honoring God or some other deity.

A *psalm*, any sacred, usually metrical song or hymn.

A *canticle*, a nonmetrical, liturgical (public and/or ritualistic) hymn, especially one from the Bible.

A *litany*, a ceremonial or liturgical prayer comprised of a series of invocations or supplications with responses that are the same for a number of stanzas in succession.

However, if you prefer to stick with the basic form of prayer, all we can say is—amen.

Dirge/Elegy/Requiem

Music may well be the "brandy of the damned," as George Bernard Shaw put it. However, it's also a source of comfort, especially when someone dies. Here are the kinds of music or poetry one might encounter at a memorial service.

When someone of stature leaves us, a *requiem (aka requiem mass)* is usually performed; it's a musical service for many voices held to honor the soul of the dead and pray for its peaceful repose.

For those who weren't a president, pope, or some such, there's a *dirge*, a short, simple funeral song, poem, or lament.

For those being honored by people who can't sing, there's an *elegy*, a poem written to praise the departed.

And where will these paeans most likely be heard? In a house of worship, at a funeral home, or outside one of these . . .

Crypt/Mausoleum/Sepulcher/Tomb/Vault

You might call this section one of grave differences. A *cemetery* and a *graveyard* are more or less synonymous, though some lexicographers define a cemetery as burial grounds *outside* a churchyard. What you might find in or about them, though, are not the same.

A *vault* is any chamber or slot therein that houses a coffin, while a *crypt* is a subterranean vault, especially one located beneath the main floor of a church. (Crypt comes from the Greek word *kryptos*, or "hidden," hence the word "cryptic.") Though *sepulcher* can be applied to any grave, it is usually used to describe a vault situated on holy ground. A *mausoleum* is a stately vault for the interment of one or more bodies.

A *tomb* is any excavation for burial, including a simple grave, but is usually used to describe one cut in rock.

GOVERNMENT

Emperor/King/Monarch/Potentate/Sovereign

During the Middle Ages, democracy was unknown to most of the world. Whoever had land had wealth, the wealthy had armies, and the armies were allied under rulers of different kinds.

A *king* (or queen) is the hereditary head of a kingdom, a state, or nation that recognizes his or her right to wield authority over them. This recognition may have been earned at swordpoint, through wisdom, or by a combination of both, but the end result is the same.

An *emperor* is the supreme ruler of an empire, which is a group of nations, clans, or even kingdoms. It, too, is a hereditary title. (In Russia, emperors were called *czars*.)

The terms *monarch* and *sovereign* are synonymous and describe either a king or an emperor. However, monarch is usually used in conjunction with "limited" and "absolute." Absolute is self-explanatory, while limited means that the ruler exercises powers under constitutional restrictions, like the present-day Queen of England.

A *potentate* can be a monarch or sovereign, but the term also describes any powerful, unelected ruler, such as an emir or a khan.

Autocrat/Demagogue

Kings and sovereigns are one kind of dictator, a hereditary leader. There are also leaders who get to the top through plotting, rhetoric, and/or opportunism.

An *autocrat* is any domineering person, usually one who wields an absolute authority that often was seized through underhanded or drastic means. Hereditary leaders may be despots, but autocrats *always* are.

A *demagogue* is also a leader, but one who has earned power and public support by arousing the emotions and frustrations of the people, usually through oratory. The term is often used as a pejorative, suggesting that an appeal to the emotions must bypass the brain, and thus is without actual merit.

Coronet/Crown/Diadem/Tiara

These days, the news is full of despots who wear helmets, berets, and other militaristic forms of head wear. In more courtly nations, however, the true sign of sovereignty or rank is still a *crown*, any kind of headgear worn in an official capacity or at a state function by a king, queen, prince, noble, etc. A crown circles the head entirely, is almost always festooned with jewels, and has a covering on top, usually of velvet or a similar fabric.

A *diadem* is a crown in the form of a band that goes around or nearly around the head and has no covering on top. It's related to a *frontal*, which is an ornamental band with a decoration on the forehead.

A *coronet* is a small crown worn by princes, nobles, or peers. It has a covering, though it's largely free of jewelry so as not to compete with the crown of a sovereign.

A *tiara* is a jeweled coronet worn by women.

Serf/Vassal

The economic, political, and social structure of Europe in the Middle Ages was known as feudalism, a system in which a serf answered to a vassal, who answered to a lord or king.

A *vassal* was an overseer, granted use of the land by a lord or king. In exchange for fealty and military service, he was allowed to keep what he grew on the land—or rather, what he had others grow, since a vassal was not one to get his hands dirty.

That was the job of the *serf*, who was virtually a slave,

a worker obliged to give service to a lord or king. His service included such wide-ranging duties as working the land to fighting wars. Beyond what the serf needed to live, anything he produced on the land was turned over to the owner. If the land was transferred or lost in combat, the serf went with it and was made to work for the land's new owner.

Not surprisingly, serfs and other peasants were a miserable lot. It wasn't until the eighteenth century that the have-nots finally began overthrowing the haves on a massive scale.

Bourgeoisie/Proletariat

Some of the greatest political upheavals in history have occurred because of dissatisfaction among the lower and middle classes. In the French Revolution, it was the *bourgeoisie* or the middle class—the shopkeepers, business-people, etc.—that overthrew King Louis XVI (and, eleven years later, ended up with a worse tyrant in the Emperor Napoléon).

In Russia, it was the even lower and more oppressed *proletariat*—the working class, especially those who had no money and had to sell their skills as laborers in order to survive—that brought down Czar Nicholas II and hoisted Lenin to power over his rivals. Ironically, the czar had been moving toward a constitutional monarchy, and, in the long run, the proletariat almost certainly would have been better off had they allowed him to remain in power.

Insurrection/Rebellion/Revolution

Why were the French and Russian upheavals called revolutions and not rebellions? It has to do with the permanence of the result.

Both are usually fought from the bottom up; that is, by the masses looking to better their lot (as opposed to a *coup d'état*, in which governmental and/or military officials conspire to wrest power from the present government).

A *rebellion* is open, armed resistance against a government or policy, staged by a small group of fanatics with the intention of winning allies and either forcing change in the existing government or establishing a new one in its place—in other words, becoming a full-fledged *revolution*, the successful overthrow of a government, and often of a form of government as well.

Typically, a rebellion implies something that is planned to a degree. An *insurrection*, however, is a rebellion that isn't necessarily planned, but is touched off by an incident and snowballs.

Hippies/Yippies

As the Russian Revolution suggests, not all revolutions end with the oppressed improving their lot. Sometimes, the most successful revolutions are those that shake up the government without overturning it.

Long before there were yuppies, buppies, and dinks there were only two kinds of "pies" in the pod. Both groups were defined in and by the 1960s, although they had somewhat different missions.

Hippies were a mid-1960s outgrowth of the beatniks of the 1950s. While the beatniks rejected the postwar values of hard work and material gain, they replaced these with a fierce devotion to art, much of which was critical of the status quo. Hippies handled disagreements with "the establishment" by protesting and/or dropping out—smoking dope or taking LSD, indulging in free love, and moving to communes.

Yippies were a radical outgrowth of hippies. In the summer of 1968, the so-called "Summer of Love," a group of activists headed by Jerry Rubin and Abbie Hoffman turned the Democratic National Convention in Chicago into an often violent forum for protest against the war in Vietnam, middle-class complacency, and police brutality. Their devoted but disorganized "Youth International Party" made a big noise and helped to accelerate the changes that occurred in the end of the decade and into the 1970s.

(Curiously, the drop-out hippies are now celebrated by history, while the overachieving yuppies of the 1980s are regarded with some disdain.)

Compact/Charter/Constitution

What's the difference between the United States Constitution, the Mayflower Compact, and the Magna Carta—the "Great Charter" signed by King John of England at Runnymede? All confer sweeping rights and liberties on the populace, although each deals with different aspects of those rights.

A *charter* is a document that confers powers and rights from the state or an organization to people, local chapters, or corporations. It validates the transfer, without going into detail about how the powers and rights are to be wielded. That's the task of . . .

The *constitution*, which is a detailed set of guidelines—a "how-to" document that sets out the laws and principles by which a government, company, or organization is to operate.

A *compact* is a little bit of both: a formal agreement between two or more parties that recognizes the rights of each and details how mutual affairs are to be conducted. A *treaty*, for example, is a compact between nations; a *contract* is a compact between two business entities.

Commonwealth/Country/Nation/Republic/State

One of the most confusing aspects of learning history in school is trying to understand why all those ancient peoples called themselves states when they were obviously nothing like California or Michigan, but were sovereign nations, and why John Wayne spoke eloquently about his love of republics in his film *The Alamo*, yet hated the Communists of Russia and its satellites—who called themselves the Union of Soviet Socialist Republics.

It's a curious state of affairs indeed.

A *state* is a group of people occupying a defined area of land, speaking the same language, and ruled by a government that was formed because of common economic, religious, or military needs. A state is made up of more than one city, though ancient city-states consisted, typically, of just one large city and the outlying areas it controlled.

A *nation* is often an outgrowth of a state or states, in

which historically unified people in the state and surrounding territories form a larger political entity. The union usually produces a depth of culture not commonly found in states.

A *country* is a nation defined geographically by its borders and physical attributes.

As for a republic, the paradox is easy to explain: the Soviets were lying. A *republic* is a state or nation in which the supreme power rests with its citizens, who are entitled to vote for representatives to carry out their will. Though the Soviets all voted, the roster of candidates was picked by the state and was thus severely limited in its choice.

A *commonwealth* is an allied group of republics, and so—for the present—at least the ex–Soviet Union got that one right.

Capital/Capitol

A vexing pair of homonyms are these two words, which come from the same Latin root, *caput*, or "head."

Capital is anything relating to the head or the uppermost part of a building, column, sentence, nation, or state, or even a financial undertaking: capital is the money used to begin a business, purchase stock, expand one's holdings in real estate, etc. (At least, capital was what businesspeople used before there was credit, but that's another matter. . . .)

Capitol, on the other hand, describes a few specific buildings. Written as Capitol, it was a Roman temple dedicated to the god Jupiter, which derived its name from its location on Capitoline Hill, where the senate regularly congregated; it is also the building that houses the Congress of the United States. Written as capitol, the word signifies any state house or house in which a state legislature sits.

Department/Division

Why is it the State Department and not the State Division? Why is a military unit a division and not a department? It's all a matter of whether the parts can function independently within the whole or whether they're more or less dependent on other parts.

A *department* is a distinct branch or section of a government, business, university, etc. It is more or less autonomous—for example, the shoe department and the jewelry department of Macy's have little to do with each other.

A *division* is a small part of a whole that is closely related to the other parts—for example, the juice division of a soda company is still dependent upon the parent company for advertising, distribution, etc.

Association/Federation/League/Organization

Though these words are frequently misused by groups looking to come up with catchy acronymns—such as the National Organization of Women, which works out better than the National Association of Women—they have specific meanings that are often intentionally overlooked.

An *organization* is an eclectic group of people, nations, parties, etc., working toward common goals, which, because of the diverse nature of the members, tend to be very broad and move forward very slowly, such as the North Atlantic Treaty Organization.

An *association* (or *society*) is a group of people who are banded together and aggressively looking out for and advancing mutual interests, such as the American Medical Association or the National Association for the Advancement of Colored People.

A *league* is an alliance of associations banded together to give them more power as they look after common interests, such as the National Baseball League or the former League of Nations.

A *federation* is a union of any of the groups above, with the distinction that while all work for the common good, each retains its autonomy and self-government—just like the Federation of *Star Trek*.

Banner/Ensign/Flag/Pennant/Standard

When you go to a sporting event, you may salute your country's flag, buy a souvenir banner, and sit under a pennant. In case you've never gone to a stadium, what you're missing are cloths emblazoned with designs, the likes of which, throughout history, have been powerful enough to stir fierce emotions, often to the point of violent death. (And those are just the *athletic* banners!)

A *flag* is a piece of cloth, usually rectangular in size, with the same design on both sides. Usually attached along one edge to a staff or cord, it is the symbol of a nation, state, or group.

A *banner* is a rectangular or triangular cloth bearing the design or motto of a party, group, athletic team, etc.

A *pennant* is a long, tapering, usually triangular cloth that is awarded for victory in athletic competition. The words banner and pennant are often used interchangeably when they symbolize schools or organizations.

If you go to a military sporting event, you will also see an *ensign* or two; these are military or naval standards indicating allegiance, affiliation, or nationality.

All of these are *standards*, physical symbols or emblems of a group, though a figure or object such as the eagle of ancient Rome or the Israeli Star of David can also be a standard.

Majority/Plurality

As anyone who follows presidential elections knows, we the people don't actually vote for presidents. We vote for a slate of electors picked by state party organizations. These electors make up the electoral college, and they choose the president by voting according to the wishes of we, the electorate. A candidate who gets 270 electoral votes—a majority—becomes president. However, a candidate who wins less than that, even if it's a plurality of electoral votes, is not automatically the winner.

A *majority* is when you win any number more than half the total—in other words, anything above fifty percent. A *plurality* is simply having won more votes than the next person or persons in line. A plurality can be a majority, but if it isn't—as can happen in the case of the electoral college—it's up to the House of Representatives to decide who lives in the White House.

Banish/Exile/Expatriate

In Edward Everett Hale's story "The Man Without a Country," treasonous U.S. naval officer Philip Nolan learns to appreciate his homeland after spending fifty-five years at sea, never visiting or hearing of his country. Now *that's* banishment. It is not, however, exile or expatriation.

To *banish* someone is to expel them from a country, and, usually, force them to live in a place not to their liking.

To *exile* someone is to force them to endure a prolonged or permanent separation from his or her country but without naming a specific place where they're to reside.

To *expatriate* is to leave a country willingly or by force *and* to discontinue being loyal to it.

Jail time is actually a form of banishment, and one possible way of getting there is to do one of the following, popular among all too many governments nowadays . . .

Cover-Up/Whitewash

The attempt to hide the Watergate break-in was a cover-up, and once the cover-up was uncovered the efforts to explain it became a whitewash. When a whitewash fails, the results are usually blackballing and prison.

A *cover-up* is simply (or not so simply, in many cases) an effort to prevent investigation or exposure of an action. That can include—but is not limited to—doctoring documents, destroying evidence, and bribery.

A *whitewash* is the use of words or actions in an effort to absolve a person or group from blame in a criminal act, scandal, etc. In other words, it's a lie. The term comes from the mixture of lime and water that at one time was used for whitening or bleaching walls and woodwork.

WEAPONS AND
THE MILITARY

Armada/Fleet/Flotilla/Navy

In history class, we're told about the Spanish Armada, but never about any other nation's armada. Did the British use one to stop the Spanish Armada? What did the Japanese have during World War II?

Technically, each of these was an *armada*, the Spanish word for a navy or fleet. However, because Phillip II ordered his Spanish Armada to attack England in 1588, the term has come to describe any large group of ships that sets out to *attack* an enemy rather than to simply defend its own shores. Given the extraordinary failure of the Spanish Armada, most sailors prefer to use the terms . . .

Fleet, the largest unit of naval ships organized for tactical purposes, though its numbers vary depending upon the theater of operations; and *flotilla*, a group of small naval vessels (there are sixteen in our own U.S. Navy, comprised of four divisions of four ships each).

In any language, a *navy* is a nation's entire body of warships: fleets, flotillas, and the officers, sailors, and yards that support them.

Pageant/Parade/Procession

Back on land, the old Ted Koehler/Harold Arlen song exclaims, "I Love a Parade," Barbra Streisand warns the world not to rain on her parade, and then there's Irving Berlin's immortal "Easter Parade." Is a parade *really* that much more exciting than a pageant or procession, which barely show up in the Tin Pan Alley catalog?

A *parade* was originally a display of military might, from the Spanish *parada*, the area in which troops exercised (and a word much better received than armada). It still means that in Spanish, but in English it came to mean any grand, strutting, colorful display that proceeds in a highly organized manner. What makes a parade so appealing is that it moves big, new elements in and out so quickly there's never a chance to get bored.

A *pageant* is a little less fleeting. Originally, it was one scene in a medieval mystery play (a play about the Bible). Later, it came to mean any elaborate or spectacular performance, usually comprised of detailed vignettes.

A *procession* isn't an entertainment of any kind: it's simply people or objects moving forward—usually in great numbers and in a narrow line—toward a destination. Whereas a parade or pageant implies "fun," a procession is typically more somber, as a funeral or religious procession.

Fort/Fortress/Stockade

With all this marching and sailing going on, warriors need a place to kick back and at the same time protect themselves from attack.

A *fort* is any strong, heavily defended place occupied by troops and usually surrounded by permanent walls. A fort is built to defend a frontier or a shore, although a city or town may rise behind it.

Conversely, a *fortress* typically *is* a small town along with its defenses. It's comprised of any number of buildings inside a wall or surrounded by a series of forts.

Fort comes from the Latin *fortis* for "strong." For fortress, the suffixes *-ar* ("pertaining to") and *-icia* ("a state or quality of being") are added.

A *stockade* is a defensive barrier or enclosure made of upright posts or timbers, erected quickly to defend newly won territory or to house troops on the move.

There are always those times in the life of fighting men and women when there just isn't time to build a fort. What to do? Grab a chair or two or three and start piling....

Barricade/Barrier

The hit musical *Les Misérables* has popularized the image of freedom fighters piled atop a barricade. It also happens to be a barrier, so why do we need two words?

Because a *barricade* is a hastily constructed barrier—as its root, *barrica*, an old Spanish word for "barrel," suggests. It's something you roll out and duck behind.

A *barrier*, from the French *barre*, a "bar," is anything constructed to prevent passage, be it a barricade or something more elaborate, such as a brick wall, a fence, or a moat.

Ninja/Samurai

From the films of Bruce Lee to the exploits of the Teenage Mutant Ninja Turtles, both the young and the old have always been fascinated by the warriors and martial arts forms of the East.

The art of *ninjutsu*—"the art of stealth"—originated approximately two thousand years ago. It was practiced by the *ninja*, men and women whose jobs were similar to those of modern-day secret agents. They were hired or retained by lords to enter enemy territory and spy, perform acts of sabotage, and assassinate rivals. Their weapons and tools included knives, throwing stars, hooks, ropes, and various poisons.

Unlike their free-lance countrymen, the *samurai*, or "guards," were members of the hereditary warrior class in feudal Japan. They were devoted to the service of a *daimyo* or "lord." Their principal weapon was a big sword known as a *katana*. The demise of the feudal system in the nineteenth century rendered the class extinct.

Cavalier/Knight/Paladin

Which came first, the horseman who became a soldier or the soldier who learned to ride? That depended on whether you were a cavalier or a knight.

A *knight*, from the Old English *cniht*, or "manservant,"

was a military servant of the king or some other feudal lord, a person permitted to hold land in exchange for serving his master as a soldier. This included—but was not limited to—fighting on horseback and protecting the ladies of the court. Later, the term came to mean anyone who had served a knight with distinction, first as a page, then as a squire, and thus rose to knighthood himself. Today, a knight is any man who, in recognition for distinguished service to Great Britain, is awarded the nonhereditary rank by the queen and is permitted to use the title "Sir."

A *paladin* was one of the twelve knights who attended Charlemagne. Today, the word means any champion.

A *cavalier*, from the Latin *caballus*, or "horse," was any horseman who took up arms, especially to serve as a lady's escort. (*Caballero*, a Spanish cavalier or gentleman, comes from the same Latin root.)

This is not to suggest that the Cavalier poets wrote on horseback. It simply means that their lyrics were distinguished by grace and wit, a mark of the cavalier.

Javelin/Lance/Spear

Here are definitions that will help clear up a few points.

A *spear* is a weapon used for throwing or thrusting. It's comprised of a wooden shaft from four to seven feet long with a pointed metal or stone tip, one that's usually shaped like an arrowhead or feather. In some civilizations, such as ancient Rome, warriors carried spears whose bottom half was wood and the rest metal. This made the spears heavier and gave them greater penetrating power when thrown than those spears that were simply metal-tipped.

A *javelin* is a light spear, just over eight feet long, usually made of wood with a metal tip that has the same circumference as the shaft and tapers to a pointed tip.

A *lance* is a shafted weapon with a pointed metal head, carried by mounted soldiers and leveled at the enemy in a charge. Short lances may be just over six feet long; long lances can be up to nine feet in length.

Ax/Hatchet/Tomahawk

You and an enemy make up: you're said to bury the hatchet. Would it also be correct to say that you bury the tomahawk? Indeed it would. In fact, it would be *more* correct, since American natives used to do just that as a gesture of reconciliation.

Both tools are members of the ax family. An *ax* is a long-handled implement for hewing and cleaving, with an iron or steel head that's bladed on one side and usually flat on the other. It's meant to be swung with two hands.

A *hatchet* is a smaller ax, able to be swung with one hand, and usually having a flattened head opposite the blade side for use as a hammer. Settlers who didn't know any better used this term to describe . . .

A *tomahawk*, a light ax with a stone or bone head sharpened on one side, used as a weapon or tool by North American Indians.

Variations on these designs include the *pick*, which has a long, narrow, pointed head or heads; the *mattock*, a long-handled tool shaped like a pick but with one broad and sharp end that is used for hacking at and loosening soil; and the *dolabra* of the ancient Romans, a long-handled weapon whose head had a pick on one side and an ax on the other.

Musket/Rifle

Back in the colonial days of America, the Revolution was helped along by the activity of militiamen known as Minutemen, who were also musketmen.

The weapon they carried, the *musket* (a word derived from the Middle French *mousquet*, a crossbow arrow), was invented in the sixteenth century. It was a heavy, large-caliber, long-barreled gun carried by soldiers and triggered, originally, by a match or matchlock (a slow-burning cord). Later, the musket was fired using a percussion lock (a hammer that struck a priming charge in a percussion cap) or a flintlock (a flint hammer used to ignite the priming charge).

Early in the nineteenth century, the musket was replaced by the *rifle* (short for *rifled gun*), the chief difference being that the rifle barrel had spiral grooves to give the ball a rotary motion and thus greater distance and accuracy. The infantry carried *military rifles*, which were long and heavy and designed to take a bayonet; smaller but otherwise identical, *carbines* were carried by the cavalry.

Dynamite/TNT

Generally, the explosives that fire a bullet from a gun, or cause larger blasts, do their job when a rapid buildup of pressure in a tight space causes gases to push their way out violently.

Although explosives had been around for hundreds of years, existing powders paled before the might of the highly explosive compound nitroglycerin, created by chemist Ascanio Sobrero in 1846. Unfortunately, the compound was unstable: a small amount of friction or a minor shock might set it off, or, conversely, it could be dropped from a rooftop and perhaps nothing would happen to it.

Inventor Alfred Nobel (of Nobel Prize fame) solved the problem by mixing nitroglycerin with kieselguhr, an absorbent, claylike earth, and triggering the mixture with a detonator or blasting cap, which was ignited by a fuse or electric current. Nobel began to manufacture thousands of tons of this mixture, *dynamite*, a year. Today, dynamite consists of from ten to thirty percent nitroglycerin, with other oxygen-rich compounds fueling the explosive mixture.

TNT—or trinitrotoluene—came about a half-century later. It's derived from toluene, a flammable liquid obtained from coal tar and petroleum. More stable than its nitroglycerin-based counterpart, TNT was used both for blasting and by the military in artillery shells (a concussion fuse would trigger the explosive when it came into contact with something solid).

Atom Bomb/Hydrogen Bomb/Neutron Bomb

Dynamite and TNT are still popular explosives among builders, miners, and the military. However, in 1945, traditional explosives were overshadowed by the dawning of the nuclear age: new bombs were measured in destructive force equal to megatons of TNT.

Yet not all such nuclear bombs are alike. An *atom bomb* (or *atomic bomb*) is a bomb whose explosive fury comes from the nuclear fission (splitting the nucleus) of atoms of U-235 or plutonium, with the conversion of part of their mass to energy.

First detonated in 1952, the *hydrogen bomb* (also *thermonuclear* or *fusion bomb*) is a more powerful bomb whose destructive force comes from the use of a fission bomb or laser to generate the heat required for the thermonuclear fusion of hydrogen (the heat-joining of the nuclei of hydrogen atoms). As a result of this fusion, heavier helium atoms are created and a vast amount of energy is released.

A more recent development is the *neutron bomb*, a small device that releases a shower of radioactive neutrons but has no explosive energy, thus killing people without destroying property.

Ah, progress.

Command/Directive/Order

You're handed a rifle and a lieutenant tells you to take a barricade. That's an *order.* You're being told to do something, but with no specific guidelines about how to do it.

You're handed a rifle and told to attack a barricade from the north side, overcoming the two rebels stationed there. That's a *command.* It implies two things: first, that what he's said will remain in force until you've succeeded, and second, that there's a specific way to do it.

If the president of the United States tells you, through channels, to take a barricade, that's a *directive.* Like the lieutenant giving orders, he doesn't care how it's done, as long as it gets done. Word to do something passed through channels from the pope, some other high-ranking figure, or—in the case of the military—from a central headquarters, would also be considered a directive.

Word from *way* high up to do something is a *commandment*—a command that is very definitely meant to be carried out.

Courier/Messenger

How do directives and orders get to the Joes and Janes in the front lines? Not by officer, that's for sure. They come by *messenger*, someone who carries papers, messages, parcels, and so forth.

On the other hand, a *courier* is a messenger who travels in haste, usually bearing diplomatic or military messages that are typically between officers or heads of state.

In ancient civilizations, messengers used to be murdered for bringing bad news to kings, generals, and other decision makers. Maybe that's how couriers came about: a messenger can learn to move awfully fast when trying to outrun a headsman.

LAW AND ORDER

Assassination/Homicide/Manslaughter/Murder

The commandments you don't want to go breaking are the Ten Commandments—especially the one that forbids *murder*, the legally or morally unjustifiable taking of a human life. (Or killing, depending upon the translation you're reading. The distinction is that even self-defense is forbidden by the "no-killing" commandment.)

If you do commit a murder, the punishment you receive in this world, at least, is determined by how and why you do it.

Homicide implies a personal and premeditated reason for killing, be it hatred, revenge, or some such. Commit a homicide, and, when the appeals process is through and unsuccessful, you may get the opportunity to join your victim.

The penalties are typically less severe for *manslaughter*, which is murder without malice or premeditation. *Involuntary manslaughter* is accidental murder; *voluntary manslaughter* is intentional murder that's provoked by "the moment"—by fear, rage, or some other overwhelming emotion.

Assassination is not necessarily the murder of someone important, as is widely presumed, although important people are often assassinated. The term means to murder by surprise or secret assault and comes from the Arabic *hashshāshīn*, or "hashish eaters," men who belonged to a secret band of Moslems that killed Christians during the Crusades. The fact that an assassin works in secret means that the subject is usually important—i.e., is constantly in view or regularly attended by assistants.

Buccaneer/Corsair/Freebooter/Pirate/Privateer

Captain Hook. Long John Silver. Edward Teach, *aka* Blackbeard. Sir Henry Morgan. Captain Blood. Jean Laffite.

Some of the most popular figures in history and fiction have been rogues of the sea, but were they pirates or something else? It depends on for whom they sailed, where they sailed, and what they did with their booty.

A *pirate* is a thief who steals on either the high seas or on the shores. In recent years, the term has come to include any plunderer or predator, such as a video pirate—though the characters played by Cyril Ritchard, Errol Flynn, and Scott Harris are still the ones that come most readily to mind when one thinks of a pirate.

A *buccaneer* is a pirate who preyed primarily on the Spanish colonies and ships in North America. The name came from the French *boucanier*, "to cure meat," which is what they did on shore before setting sail with the meat on what were often long voyages.

A *corsair* sailed in a different bailiwick: he looted the Barbary Coast, usually in fast ships also called corsairs, from which the passengers took their name.

A *freebooter* was originally a Dutch pirate *(vrijbuiter)* who went anywhere and everywhere in search of plunder. The term soon came to describe any pirate who worked for hire.

A *privateer* was the only kind of pirate motivated by reasons other than greed. Like Geoffrey Thorpe in the film *The Sea Hawk*, a privateer worked on behalf of the government to harass enemy ships. If captured, he was expected to disavow any connection with the government.

Which just goes to show that one person's pirate can be another person's hero.

Arsonist/Pyromaniac

Arsonists and pyromaniacs are frequently killers by virtue of what they do. But while they're both colloquially referred to as firebugs, these two have entirely different reasons for setting fires.

An *arsonist* is someone who burns property he or she owns, or property that belongs to another, out of malice or for the insurance. However wrong or illegal, there is a specific motive behind what the arsonist does.

A *pyromaniac* is someone who has a compulsion to set fires, period. There may be a pattern to the fires, and the pyromaniac may have a sophisticated knowledge of the process of setting different kinds of fires—more than simply lighting a match. However, the crimes are without any motive beyond the mania itself.

Assault/Battery

In law, these are usually lumped together because one frequently leads to the other—and to lumps.

Assault is a threat or an unsuccessful attempt to cause physical harm to someone else (in law, *mens rea*, "the intent to commit a crime").

Battery is making good on the threat or attempt, and actually using force against another person—either with the hands or with an object of some kind (in law, this is *actus reus*, "a criminal act," and is known to be perpetrated against in-laws).

Though it might seem odd at first, the etymology of battery makes sense: it comes from the Old French *battre*, "to beat." How, then, did the electric battery come to be named? Because soldiers used to batter the enemy with a series of weapons or *batteries*. The word came to apply to any series of objects working toward a similar goal, which the galvanic cells of a battery certainly do.

Burglary/Larceny/Robbery

Frequently, assault and battery are part of another crime, especially one of these.

Robbery is to appropriate something from a person or premises with the use or threat of force. *Larceny* is the same thing, though there are two gradations: *grand larceny* is the theft of something valued at more than fifty dollars, while *petty larceny* is a small theft.

Burglary has always been defined as breaking into a house at night with the intent to steal when the occupants are abed or away. However, today most states define it as breaking into any place at any time for the purpose of robbing it.

These crimes are considered *felonies*—major crimes that are usually punishable with prison or death, as opposed to minor crimes, or *misdemeanors*.

Dope/Drug

One of the reasons so many people get into crime in the first place is to obtain money, so they can buy one or the other of these.

The word "drug" comes from the old Dutch word *droog*, meaning "dried," and was applied to any dry substance such as herbs that were used for medicinal purposes.

Around the turn of the century, *drug* took on its secondary, nonmedicinal meaning, used to describe any habit-forming, deteriorative and/or hallucinogenic, usually self-prescribed substance, from nicotine to heroin.

Since circa 1870, *dope* has been used by drug addicts to describe any narcotic, nonprescribed drug, such as opium, because it makes the user "dopey."

Defamation/Libel/Slander

In the old days, men who were insulted by their peers challenged them to a duel and the matter was settled on the field of honor. Today, it's settled in a court of law.

Defamation is a broad term that includes both libel and slander: it's false or unwarranted injury caused to the reputation of another.

Libel is a published or broadcast remark about an individual that is injurious to his or her reputation and is *also* demonstrably false. *Slander* is oral character assassination—i.e., words spoken in an auditorium, at a rally, etc. A magazine that reports slander and in so doing repeats it may be found liable for libel.

It's up to the courts to determine the difference between

defamation and *criticism*, which is a person's fair and legitimate appraisal of the work of another.

Copyright/Patent/Registration/Trademark

Criticism and other forms of intellectual property, artistic expression, inventions, etc., are protected by the law in various ways.

Suppose you decide to publish a comic book called *Tiger-Man.* Your subtitle is, "He Gives Criminals No-Escape Claws." Your story: Dr. Lancaster Hill goes to Africa, conducts research in the wild, and accidentally injects himself with tiger blood, thus obtaining the powers and abilities of a big cat.

The story you come up with can be *copyrighted,* albeit just for a period of your, the author's, lifetime plus fifty years. You can't legally protect the idea that a doctor injected with animal blood is endowed with the powers of that animal: you couldn't stop a competitor from coming out with *Giraffe-Man,* or, depending on the mood of the court, even *Tiger-Woman* or *Tiger-Boy* (which is why the copyright holders of Batman came up with Batwoman, Batgirl, Man-Bat, and even Bat-Hound, although they obviously felt that baseball had a lock on Batboy). A copyright also doesn't protect from someone summarizing the story in a nonfiction work, as we've done here. Only the distinctive details and unique expression of your story can't be used by someone else.

The name Tiger-Man and his alter ego are *trademarks,* distinctive names, designs, and other elements used to distinguish your character from Superman, Spider-Man, and others. A little *TM* in a circle indicates that the material beside it is your trademark, and you'll protect it in court if need be. Keep in mind, though, that if someone set up a 900 number and asked callers, "What do you think of Tiger-Man?" you could not stop them. No trademark violation is committed if using the name is the only practical way to identify it—provided that no sponsorship or endorsement of a product is implied.

A small *R* in a circle means that you've gone through the trouble of sending the material to the U.S. Patent and

Trademark Office in Washington and obtained a fancy document of *registration*; this adds little to your legal hold on the property other than to show potential infringers that you spent money getting it and thus you *really* mean business.

A little *SM* in a circle beside the phrase "He Gives Criminals No-Escape Claws" indicates that this is your *service mark*, a phrase that uniquely expresses your trademarked property or business concept—for example, a Tiger-Man "Earn Your Stripes Club" for readers.

The individual property aside, the name of your new company, Atlas Periodicals, is an incorporated *trade name*, while the words Atlas Comic Books or Heroic Comic Books or whatever, on the top of the cover, is a descriptive *brand name*—although the distinctive design of any ACB logo would be a trademark.

Except for the copyright, all of the above are renewable in perpetuity. Thus, even when the original Tiger-Man story goes out of copyright, a competitor wouldn't be able to reprint it because the costume, logo, etc., are still protected.

The only way a *patent* would apply to any of these is if you invented a new type of printing press or some other mechanical invention or physical process of doing something. A computer program to draw the comics would be copyrightable; the hardware itself would be patentable. Generally, patents are issued for seventeen years without chance for renewal.

Copyright Infringement/Plagiarism

When a filmmaker shoots a scene exactly as another filmmaker did it, it's a homage. When John F. Kennedy said in his inaugural address, "Ask not what your country can do for you—ask what you can do for your country," he was paying tribute to the same sentiment that was expressed in the funeral oration for John Greenleaf Whittier. However, when the chunk of material being appropriated is longer and more substantial than these, new definitions come into play.

Copyright infringement is the reproduction of a work or a substantial portion thereof without permission of the copyright holder—for example, copying a videotape or even photocopying sections of, say, a management book to distribute to executives in a company. Parody (see entry, below) is not copyright infringement.

Plagiarism is the theft of the ideas, thoughts, and/or words of another and representing them as one's own. This might be a form of copyright infringement—for instance stealing the plot of a novel, even though most of the words are new, or incorporating several bars of music into an otherwise new composition; or it might be legal but just plain bad form, such as paraphrasing sections of someone else's ideas in a speech, paper, or other work.

Obscene/Pornographic

A XXX film called *The Sexorcist* would probably be considered a parody of *The Exorcist*, so the filmmakers would be off the hook where copyright infringement is concerned.

As to whether the film would be considered obscene or pornographic, the Supreme Court has left these definitions to "community standards." Though that constitutes a legal twilight zone, pornography and obscenity *are* definable lexicographically. (Or, as Bertrand Russell put it, "Obscenity is whatever happens to shock some elderly and ignorant magistrate.")

A text, picture, movie, etc., is *pornographic* if its primary intent is to arouse sexual desire. A work of artistic merit may have explicit sexual elements without being considered pornographic—for example, the writings of Anaïs Nin or Bernardo Bertolucci's film *Last Tango in Paris*. Such works are more accurately described as *erotic*.

However, those same works can be described as *obscene*, a more subjective term meaning something that is offensive to the sense of modesty or decency of a person or community. "Curse words" and graphic photographs of a homicide victim can also be described as obscene, and the latter might be considered pornographic as well if the viewer is sexually aroused by violence.

Testament/Will

In the old days, as far back as the ancient Greeks, a will and testament were very nearly identical: the contents were the same, with the only difference being that a will was written in one's own hand while a testament was written in the hand of another.

Today they're different things, though where there's a will, there's a testament.

A *will* is the legal statement of a person's wishes regarding the disposal of his or her estate and of other matters to be performed after death.

A *testament* is the section of a will that relates solely to the disposition of property.

It should come as no surprise that as soon as civilization reached a point where people had to make out wills, there was someone there to lend a hand, literally and figuratively. . . .

Barrister/Solicitor

In the United States, whether you're a lawyer, an attorney, or a counselor, your job is to prepare legal documents, advise clients, and represent them if need be in the lowest courts to the highest.

In England, though, there are two kinds of lawyers, both of whom practice at different levels. The lowest (level, not lawyer) is a *solicitor*, who is sanctioned by the Inns of Court to draw up papers, advise clients on the law, represent them before the lower courts, and also work on preparing cases for . . .

A *barrister*, a higher-flying legal eagle who pleads cases in the superior courts. Barristers are so lofty, in fact, that they usually aren't hired by ordinary blokes but by solicitors.

In Scotland, barristers are called *advocates*.

Barrister comes from the word "bar," to which legal representatives in England and the U.S. must be admitted before they can practice law. The term derives from the railings in old English courts that used to separate the public from the counselors, judge, and jury.

Incidentally, there is no difference between an American *lawyer* or *attorney*; a *counselor* usually refers to a trial lawyer.

Grand Jury/Jury

It always sounds so ominous when someone is hauled before a grand jury—probably because that name makes it seem really important. Well, it *is*, but the truth is, a grand jury is convened simply to see if there's any reason for a person to actually go on trial before a jury.

A *grand jury* is a group of twelve to twenty-three ordinary citizens brought together to hear a prosecutor and determine if there is sufficient evidence to warrant an indictment. If there is, criminal charges are pressed, a trial date is set, and a *jury* (*aka* a *petit jury*) is convened, consisting of six to twelve citizens, plus one to three alternates (if the trial is expected to be long and complex). The jury listens to the prosecution and defense at the trial and eventually determines the guilt or innocence of a defendant.

Trials are held to examine the evidence. And throughout history, if things didn't work out well for the defendant, one of the following entries awaited. . . .

Fetter/Manacle/Shackle

In the days before we learned how to work with bronze, people who broke tribal laws or offended their rulers were bound with hemp and lashed to a tree or rock. Metalworking brought a more effective—though not more humane—means of restraining lawbreakers, but it wasn't until the late twentieth century that lightweight metals and plastics were invented to make life easier for prisoners while they're being transported to court or between prisons.

In general, there are two kinds of restraints.

A *shackle* is any metal restraint (usually an iron ring) fastened to the hands, feet, waist, or neck. Chains are run between the shackles and/or to an object such as a ball or a wall to restrict movement.

A *manacle* is a shackle for the hand that is usually heavier than handcuffs; a *fetter* (or, more commonly, *fetters*) is a shackle for the feet.

And where do these manacled convicts end up? That depends on the state of their case.

Jail/Prison

In October of 1931, a headline of the *Chicago Sunday Tribune* read: CAPONE IN JAIL; PRISON NEXT.

Isn't that a redundancy? What's next for the *Tribune*— DEWEY DEFEATS TRUMAN?

Actually, the newspaper was correct (about Capone, not Dewey). Except for the fact that both are cells, a jail and a prison aren't the same thing.

A *jail* is a place where people awaiting trial are detained, or where those convicted of minor offenses—usually those of thirty days or under—are kept. Husbands who fail to pay child support and reporters who refuse court orders to turn over their notebooks are also sent to jail.

A *prison*, on the other hand, is a facility where those found guilty of major crimes are taken to serve out their term (time spent in jail is almost always subtracted from a convict's prison sentence). A prison is also known as a *penitentiary*, where, in theory at least, criminals do penance.

In Britain, officials still use the spelling *gaol* instead of jail (they're pronounced the same), though the latter is used by journalists.

Pillory/Stocks

Until the early 1800s, prison was considered too good for some criminals. For them, only public humiliation in stocks or pillories was a suitable form of punishment.

Stocks were wooden devices consisting of an upper and lower slabs, which, when closed, formed two holes. A seated prisoner's feet were placed within while the device was still open; when it was padlocked shut, the prisoner's ankles were trapped rather snuggly in the holes.

A *pillory* was a wooden frame that worked on the same

principle, only it held the hands, and, unfortunately, usually the head of a prisoner who was standing.

Both devices were invented some time in the Middle Ages. Of the two, the pillory was the more severe form of punishment. If victims were too short, they might suffocate as they hung by their head; even if they were able to stand, they might suffer more punishment according to the whims of the crowd. Rarely did authorities intervene when mobs gathered and pelted a prisoner with vegetables and eggs—which were rotten and usually sold at nearby stands—mud, or even stones. Officers of the court could be paid to stick around and wipe the captive's face; otherwise, suffocation was common.

Much to the chagrin of prosecutors, stocks and pillories weren't always successful forms of punishment. For example, when author Daniel Defoe was pilloried for having attacked the Church of England in his writings, the sympathetic public festooned his head with flowers. And when a publisher was pilloried for printing a book unfavorable to King George III, the public filled the man's hat with a total of two hundred guineas.

BUSINESS AND COMMERCE

Career/Livelihood/Profession/Trade/Vocation

The buzzword of the eighties was *career*. What the yuppies, buppies, dinks, students, and the rest of the go-getters were worried about was their life's work and the course it would take. But career is a broad term comprised of several elements, including one or more of the following:

A *livelihood*, or the means by which you earn money—the kind of job you do. This can change from day to day, which makes it less specific than . . .

An *occupation*, your steady or principal line of work or business. If you're involved in an occupation that requires a limited amount of training in one area, then you have a *trade*—for example, a housepainter or fast-food cook.

If you have an occupation that requires extensive training and usually some education in addition to training, you're following a *vocation*—for instance, plumbing or auto repair.

If your occupation requires extensive education, then it's your *profession*—such as medicine, accounting, the law, etc.

And if you're reading this on the job (unless you're the book's editor), then you'll soon be *unemployed*.

Archetype/Prototype

You're a toymaker, and you've just finished designing a game called Wall Street. When the game is sold in stores, the playing pieces representing brokers, yuppies, judges, etc., will be made of plastic; for now, you're using tokens fashioned from clay. Eventually, game cards and play money will be printed; the ones you're using now are drawn on index cards and slips of paper with Magic Marker.

The fully conceptualized game before you is the *prototype*, an original model or perfectly realized pattern for the finished item.

You sell the game to a manufacturer, who hires an artist to draw the board and the finished illustrations for the cards. A sculptor refines the clay pieces, makes a mold, and produces a set of plastic pieces. The game is virtually indistinguishable from the product as it will finally be released. This is the *archetype*, the definitive form from which all things of the same kind are made.

Unfortunately, the game comes out and bombs because this is the era of electronics. You go back to the drawing board to revise your game, and the first question you must face is whether to redesign it as a video game or as a computer game. . . .

Arcade Game/Computer Game/Video Game

In 1974, when the electronic game "Pong" hit arcades and hotel lobbies nationwide, a new industry was born. Soon, we were able to play all kinds of electronic games for a quarter: "Space Invaders," "Pac-Man," "Donkey Kong," and many more. Simplified versions of these arcade games were made for the home market via systems such as Atari, Odyssey, Astrocade, Intellivision, and Colecovision.

At the same time, these games, as well as role-playing adventures, chess, and other programs, were created for the burgeoning home computer market.

Nearly twenty years later, arcade games, computer games, and video games are still with us, though they differ in several ways.

Arcade games are self-contained units consisting of a sophisticated program stored on chips and hooked to a monitor, sound system, and controls, and housed in a stand-alone unit. Some of these games are modular, meaning that arcade operators can change the game by inserting a different computer board or boards into the unit. This is obviously less expensive for both manufacturer and operator, since the entire game doesn't have to be shipped back to the factory.

Video games are generated by computer chips packaged inside a cartridge, which is plugged into a console hooked to a TV. Because there's less storage space in a cartridge than on an arcade board, video-game programs tend to feature sophisticated graphics processors that generate fast, colorful graphics. Game-play options are relatively limited, but things move too quickly for most players to care.

Computer games are written on diskettes and run on personal computers. Typically, personal computers have a fair amount of general purpose hardware, and the software is written accordingly: animation is usually limited, but the narratives tend to be much more intricate and interactive. For example, for many adventure games, the player can type instructions on the keyboard and the game will respond, in type, on the screen. Video games let you punch in codes, and that's generally it.

Attaché Case/Briefcase

If you're a businessperson or professional, you need something to carry around your important papers—though more often than not, that means newspapers and a bag lunch.

A sandwich and an apple won't fit very well in an *attaché case*, a thin case with square corners and rigid sides used, once, by diplomatic officials and originally called a *dispatch case*. They've been in use since the early 1800s and gave rise to . . .

The *briefcase*, a flat, rectangular case, often with rounded corners. Originally made of leather and used by lawyers in the middle 1800s for carrying briefs, the briefcase was later adopted by officials and businesspeople.

Today, both attaché cases and briefcases are made of various materials, though the former are always thin and shaped in the traditional way, while briefcases come in various shapes, sizes, and depths.

Shop/Shoppe/Store

From their titles, you can tell that films like *The Shop on Main Street* and *Little Shop of Horrors* are going to have an intimate air about them—certainly more so than *Little Store of Horrors*. That's because a shop *is* a more intimate place.

Shop comes from the Old English *sceoppa*, which was a stall or booth at a fair. Today, it's a place of small-to-medium size where you can buy goods at retail prices. The word frequently suggests that the goods being sold were made there, such as a flower shop, candy shop, etc.

Store comes from the Latin *instaurare*, which is "to set up"—in this case, to set up goods for sale. A store can be any size, but the word is usually applied to an outlet of considerable size that offers more than one kind of item—for example, a grocery store or clothing store.

A *shoppe*—originally the English spelling of shop—is now used to describe a very small shop, usually devoted to one kind of product such as lingerie, art books, etc.

Duty/Tariff

Compared to the American colonists, we've got it easy where taxes are concerned. Back then, taxes—in particular, tariffs—were so high that they helped spur the American Revolution.

The colonists were reasonable folks willing to pay a reasonable *duty*, a flat tax imposed by the government on imports or exports, usually based on the item's dollar value. But a *tariff* was more, a list or table describing multiple duties due on specific items.

For example, merchants importing or exporting cloth would pay a duty on the fabric, while merchants importing or exporting finished clothing would also have to pay a duty on thread, buttons, etc., instead of a flat duty on the whole garment. The tariff schedule allowed the tax collector to compute the full amount due.

Often, a tariff was levied on the same item in both ports. Not only were the rates in Europe lower, but the colonies weren't as well-equipped to produce finished goods, so their tariffs were especially high. What's more, the colonists had no say in how they were levied, leading to the famous Revolutionary rallying cry, "No taxation without representation."

Good thing we've got representation today to keep our taxes down.

Guarantee/Warranty

We guarantee you'll only want warranties after you compare the two.

When you buy an appliance and the dealer gives you a *guarantee*, you're getting the dealer's assurance that you'll be happy with the product or service and that what you're buying will perform as advertised, or your money will be cheerfully refunded. But while guarantees are usually in writing, they tend to be generalized and full of loopholes. In short, they're only as good as the seller's word.

A *warranty*, on the other hand, is a legal contract from the manufacturer or dealer that spells out exactly what their responsibilities are regarding the parts, costs, dates of coverage, exemptions, etc. You may not like all the terms—but at least you'll know where you stand!

Estimate/Guesstimate

Businesspeople put one of these two words on the lexical map in the 1980s, and the too cute neologism is still with us, stronger than ever.

Guesstimate first appeared in the early 1960s and gained in popularity during the fast-moving eighties. People who didn't have time to do research and make calculations were asked to give an educated guess—a guesstimate.

Estimate, on the other hand, comes from the estimable Latin word *aestimare*, "to value," and means to form an opinion or judgment based on approximate calculations. To make an estimate takes time; the more time spent collecting data, the more precise the estimate will be.

Since time is money, guesstimate is here to stay, along with all the quality it implies.

EDUCATION

Alibi/Excuse

When you end up in the principal's office for one infraction or another, the first thing out of your mouth is usually an apology, followed by one of these.

An *excuse* is an explanation you tender for having failed to honor a promise, responsibility, or obligation. It may be embellished by circumstantial evidence (teeth marks on your hand from when you tried to pull the book report free of the dog's jaws), but it's still unwitnessed. An excuse does not demand proof, just credibility. As Kipling wrote in "The Lesson," "We have forty million reasons for failure, but not a single excuse."

On the other hand (the one without the tooth marks), an *alibi* is an explanation regarding your whereabouts when you were supposed to be someplace else; in law, it's proof that you were not present when a crime was being committed. An alibi requires a witness, a visa, or some other theoretically incontrovertible evidence.

Didactic/Pedantic

A mind is a terrible thing to waste, but a wasted mind does not necessarily mean a mind that's empty. It can also be a mind crammed with . . .

The *pedantic*, an excessive or inappropriate show of learning and scholarship, usually emphasizing unnecessary details. It's fine to know the names of all the presidents of the United States, but it's hollow pedantry to know how Adams County, Nebraska, voted in 1976. (For Gerald Ford, as it happens.)

Lessons that are *didactic* focus on useful, instructive information, though they tend to be preachy and moralizing as well. A sermon that illuminates a section of the Bible while at the same time underscoring its ethical lessons is didactic.

Thanks to the first paragraph above, this entry is didactic.

Academic/Scholastic

As you sat there taking those dreadful exams called Scholastic Aptitude Tests, your brow moist with sweat as you searched through all the stores of pedantic and didactic information in your noggin, did you ever stop to wonder why they weren't called Academic Aptitude Tests?

We didn't think so. Here, then, is the reason.

According to definitions cooked up in academia, *scholastic* pertains to those purely factual intellectual pursuits you follow in school, from history to science to English.

Academic, on the other hand, embraces idea-driven studies rather than those that are fact-driven—for example, literature and philosophy. (Which is why the term "it's academic" applies to a situation where you know what to do but are powerless to put it into effect. Ideas without the means to implement them are helpless.)

What's ironic is that of all the places of higher learning, an academy is the least academic institution you can attend. . . .

Academy/College/University

Academy is derived from the name Akadēmos, the Greek gentleman at whose estate Athenian thinkers would meet to teach and exchange ideas. The word initially was used to describe any group of authorities in a given field; later on it was taken to mean a high school (usually a private one). It still means that today, although it can also be used to describe any secondary school (high school) or postsecondary school where a general but intensive education is provided. It differs from a *vocational school* in that the latter tends to

59

emphasize specific areas of study and prepares students for a trade.

College is a postsecondary school where a general or liberal arts education is offered, though, like the academy of Akadēmos, it can also indicate a group of experts or kindred professionals who have a shared duty, such as the College of Cardinals or the electoral college.

A *university* is a postsecondary school that comprises a college, offers graduate studies, and in most cases has institutes (see entry, below) and professional schools for doctors, lawyers, etc.

You might say there's quite a degree of difference between them all!

Foundation/Institute/Institution

Despite the similarity of the words, there's a world of difference between an institute and an institution, though those who attend the former might disagree.

An *institute* is a place of learning that generally, concentrates on a specific field—such as computer technology or music. Typically it is attached to a university.

An *institution* is a totally independent establishment devoted to the promotion and/or study of social causes, educational subjects, cultural affairs, or various kinds of afflictions. The money to run an institution comes from grants and tuition.

A *foundation* is simply a fully endowed institution.

Pupil/Scholar/Student

Whether you're attending a college, university, or institute, you and your classmates will be students or scholars, but never pupils.

A *pupil* is a young person who is a member of a class and studies under the supervision of a teacher. The term generally applies to a child in elementary school; his or her relative youth is represented by the Latin root of pupil, *pūpus* ("boy") and *pūpa* ("girl").

A *student* is a person who is taught at an institution of

secondary or higher learning, also in a class and by a teacher. The word can also apply to one who is engaged in formal or informal independent research—for example, a student of human nature. The word student derives from the Latin root *studēre*, "to take pains."

People who study with tutors are referred to as students, while those who study music are pupils, since most people begin such studies as children.

Although *scholar* can be used to describe any pupil or student, it is correctly applied to an advanced student studying in a specialized and/or intellectually demanding area, *or* one whose merit has entitled him or her to receive financial aid.

Podium/Rostrum

Hopefully, you won't fall prey to any slips of the tongue if you're invited to one of these.

If you're asked to step to a lectern, you're going up to a stand with a slanted top where you can place your book, notes, music, etc. But if the lectern's on a podium or rostrum, would you know how to tell the two apart?

A *podium* is a small, simple platform on which a speaker or conductor stands.

A *rostrum* is also a platform for public speaking, but it's generally larger than a podium and usually has decorations on the sides or corners, a holdover from when ancient Roman commanders used to advertise their triumphs by adorning platforms with beaklike sections from the prows of captured warships.

MATH AND SCIENCE

Conundrum/Enigma/Puzzle/Riddle

Albert Einstein once wrote, "Out yonder there is a huge world, which exists independent of us human beings and which stands before us like a great, eternal riddle, at least partially accessible to our inspection and thinking."

As Einstein suggests, most of math and science involves problems to be solved, whether it's computing the distance of a newly discovered quasar or predicting the effects of acid rain on a field. The bulk of these problems take one of four forms.

A *puzzle* is a confusing question or situation, the answer to which must be discerned by putting together available or accessible pieces of information. For instance: To figure out why birds migrate to warmer climates, you must find out about bird anatomy, what happens to their food supply in the winter, whether predators move in to chase them out, and so forth.

A *riddle* is a puzzle whose answer depends upon a pun or wordplay. For example: "I'll be arriving in town when a youngster goes to the dentist. What time is that?" (Answer: Tooth hurty). A *conundrum* is a more complex problem—for example, the Sphinx's question to Oedipus: "What walks on four legs in the morning, two in the afternoon, and three in the evening?" (Answer: A man—as a baby, as an adult, and using a cane.) Its answer need not depend on a pun or wordplay.

An *enigma* is an even deeper puzzle—typically about an individual, although it can also pertain to situations—about which much more must be learned before understanding can be achieved. Unlike a puzzle, an enigma may prove to be unsolvable. For example, the existence and fate of the continent of Atlantis remain an enigma to us.

The way we solve any kind of puzzle is through logic or reason . . . although the results we get from each may vary!

Logic/Reason

Logic is the process of drawing a reliable conclusion based on facts that are known in a given situation. Speculation doesn't ever enter into the equation.

Reason seeks to elaborate on what is known through facts by "argument," either with oneself or with another. Though in theory it's as equally dispassionate, reason can lead to a wrong conclusion, whereas logic, when fastidiously applied, cannot. However, reason's prized quality is that it enables us to blaze trails into areas where there aren't sufficient facts to guide us.

Does that make *Star Trek*'s Captain Kirk a deeper thinker than Mr. Spock? Reason it out. And while you're doing that, here are both qualities in action. . . .

Hypothesis/Theory

In 1905, when our friend Mr. Einstein put forth his thoughts and conclusions on relativity, it was designated a theory. Obviously, Einstein was very sure of himself.

How do we know that? Because a *theory* is a group of propositions used to explain specific phenomena, and, while it's conjectural, it's highly educated conjecture, based solidly on fact and arrived at primarily through logic. In other words, it's the result of study.

A *hypothesis* is also a set of propositions used to explain specific phenomena. However, the base of facts from which a hypothesis is derived is less than that of a theory. Thus, a hypothesis relies on many more presumptions than a theory. In other words, it's a guideline for study.

English biologist T. H. Huxley correctly defined the limitations of both theories and hypotheses when he wrote, "The chess-board is the world; the pieces are the phenomena of the universe; the rules of the game are what we call the laws of Nature." All of which can be put another way: The name of the game is the cosmos.

Cosmos/Universe

Why did Carl Sagan call his PBS series *Cosmos* instead of *Universe*? Because he was concerned not just with all the things that are out there, but with how they relate to one another.

The *Universe* describes the totality of the matter that exists throughout space: planets, pulsars, superstrings, black holes, you name it.

The *Cosmos* refers to the universe as a harmonious and orderly system: it's not just the heavenly bodies, but how they're organized, how they interrelate, and how they evolve.

Which is why, one supposes, we have a Miss Universe Pageant and not a Miss Cosmos Pageant: would the viewing audience really care about a contestant's center of gravity or Doppler shift? (Though even Miss Universe is an egotistic misnomer, as ours is the only world represented!)

Meteoroid/Meteor/Meteorite

Few sights in the nighttime sky are as thrilling as a shooting star, although the name is as misleading as any in our language.

First off, a piece of space rock or grain drifting through the universe is a *meteoroid*.

When a meteoroid intercepts our planet—as 100,000 tons do to our earth every year—and zips through the atmosphere, it burns up from the heat of the friction, leaving a bright, short-lived tail in its wake. This streak of light is a *meteor*, *aka* a "shooting star." (The rock itself is still a meteoroid.) Each year, the earth's orbit passes through over a dozen streams of meteoroids, resulting in spectacular late night displays.

When a portion of the meteor survives and hits the ground, that fragment is called a *meteorite*. Don't be fooled by that diminutive "-ite" suffix, though: some meteorites weigh as much as sixty tons!

Mass/Weight

Mass is the amount of matter in a body—or, technically speaking, how much effort is required to put the body into motion or to stop it once it is in motion. Mass determines the density of an object: the more mass there is in one object compared to another of the same size, the denser it is. Thus an ounce of molten steel is denser than an ounce of water.

Weight is simply the force that gravity exerts upon a body. Obviously, an object with greater mass will weigh more than an object with less mass.

Weight changes from place to place, depending upon gravity, while mass does not. A person standing on the moon will weigh one-sixth as much on the earth, but the person's mass will not change.

Gamma Rays/X Rays

Physical bodies like meteoroids, moons, and human beings represent the visible side of the universe. But there's an invisible side as well, consisting of forces such as gravity and waves of light and other forms of radiation. For instance . . .

We know that X rays enable doctors to take pictures of our insides, and that gamma rays turned Bruce Banner into the Incredible Hulk. But is that all that sets them apart?

X rays are the same kind of electromagnetic radiation as light, but of a much shorter wavelength. They occur when a stream of electrons encounters atoms, knocking away the orbiting electrons and taking their place. As this replacement occurs, the incoming electrons give off energy in the form of X rays.

The denser an object struck by X rays, the more radiation it absorbs; thus, bones show up on X-ray photographs while flesh, which has little density, does not. These rays were discovered by Wilhelm Röntgen in 1895, who used *X* to describe the initially little understood nature of the rays.

Gamma rays are also electromagnetic radiation, but of an even shorter wavelength. They're emitted by the nuclei of radioactive atoms such as uranium or radium during decay—that is, during the transformation of unstable particles into more stable ones (for example, a neutron becoming a proton).

"Gamma" was used because the first two letters of the Greek alphabet had already been taken (alpha to describe rays consisting of a stream of neutrons and protons; beta to describe a flow of electrons or positrons).

Alas, though the Hulk-making capacity of gamma rays is nil, they *might* make you green ... of the very unpleasant, glow-in-the-dark kind.

Fluorescence/Incandescence/Luminescence/Phosphorescence

While we're on the subject of radiation, here's an entry in a lighter vein, starting with what happens when an object is exposed to X rays or some other form of stimulus.

The result is *fluorescence*, an emission of visible light. When the source is removed, the fluorescence dies. A fluorescent light is a tube coated with a fluorescent substance that glows when hit with electrons from within; a fluoroscope is a fluorescent screen that glows when struck by X rays or some other form of radiation, thus allowing doctors, for example, to see live images from inside the body.

Incandescence is the creation of light by high temperatures, such as the light a filament emits when it's heated by the electricity inside a light bulb.

Luminescence is the emission of light at temperatures below that of incandescence. In other words, it's cold light. One type of luminescence is *phosphorescence*, in which a substance emits light after having absorbed light or radiation from another source. Unlike fluorescence, however, phosphorescence may continue for a while after the source of excitation has been removed.

Current/Voltage

Many kinds of light are generated by electricity, and the amount of power it takes to run them is measured in watts. A watt is a current of one ampere flowing across a potential difference of one volt.

Which means *what*, exactly?

Electricity is energy caused by the motion of electrons, protons, and other particles. *Current* is simply the movement or flow of electricity, the levels of which are measured in amperes.

Voltage is the electromotive force or "potential difference" needed to move current through a conductor. The amount of voltage required depends upon the conductor's resistance, or, in other words, anything that obstructs the passage of the current and transforms electricity into heat.

We can *see* light and *feel* electricity. Now, what about a kind of wave we can *hear*? . . .

Echo/Reverberation

Here's something you may not have known.

We repeat: Here's something you may not have known. And the good news is, it's easier to grasp than the inner workings of the atom.

If a sound bounces once, it's an *echo*—the repetition of a sound that's produced by the reflection of sound waves from an obstructing surface.

If a sound bounces back more than once, that's *reverberation.*

The concept of reverberation has been adapted to other areas such as history, in which events are said to reverberate through time. What this means is that the original event is still discernible in that which it eventually causes—for example, the Civil War and its effects make an impact on current civil rights policies.

Numbers/Numerals

"Your days are numbered!" the policeman shouts to the crook, his words echoing through the alleyway.

Why are the crook's days numbered instead of numeraled (apart from the fact that the building is surrounded)? Because *number* is a unit of quantity indicating an amount; the days remaining for the criminal's illegal activities have a fixed limit—in this case, zero.

Each and every number has a specific relationship with other such units, be it an integer (whole number), a fraction, a cardinal number (expressing an amount, such as one, two, three . . .), or an ordinal number (expressing a degree or position, such as first, second, third . . .).

A *numeral* is something different. It's the actual symbol or word used to express a number. This is the reason we call them Roman numerals instead of Roman numbers (although the Romans' numbers were the same as ours).

Of course, when the police get that aforementioned criminal to jail and stamp a big 72575 on his back, he himself is now a number who is numeraled. . . .

Arithmetic/Mathematics

Of course, you don't have to be a lawbreaker for your days to be numbered. Ours are, all the time. From morning to night, we turn to numbers in our work, personal finances, cooking, and more. But when we do that, are we relying on arithmetic or on mathematics?

Usually both, since one is a subdivision—as it were—of the other. The roots of the words tell most of the story: both come from the Greek, *arithmētikós* ("of numbers") and *mathēmatikē* ("scientific craft").

Arithmetic is the foundation of mathematics. It's computation with numbers—basically addition, subtraction, multiplication, and division—and the laws that apply to them.

Mathematics is the larger picture, the use of numbers and/or symbols to express or compute relationships between figures and forms, to figure out differences between quantities, and so on.

Examples of mathematics include . . .

Algebra/Calculus/Geometry/Trigonometry

Algebra is the branch of mathematics dealing with the properties of, and relationships between, quantities and amounts, often using letters and symbols to represent or express values and numbers.

Calculus is a form of mathematical problem-solving divided into two primary forms: differential calculus (dealing with continuously varying quantities and their relationship to constants); and integral calculus (which involves computing area and volume).

Geometry is the mathematical study of the relationships between points, lines, figures, and solids.

Trigonometry deals with the relations between the sides and angles of various kinds of triangles. These relationships, known as trigonometrical ratios, can be used to help solve numerous mathematical problems.

Mastering these disciplines is difficult, but the logic and reason they require help us in other areas of our lives. The value of education is not to teach us facts per se, but to teach us to think.

Which dovetails nicely into . . .

LETTERS

Gerund/Participle

Those pesky "-ing" words.

One distinction no one but an English teacher (or should that be "-inglish" teacher?) seems to be able to remember is the one between gerund and participle. Both are verbals—verbs used as some other part of speech—but they're different kinds of verbals.

A *gerund* is a noun form of a word derived from a verb and ending in "-ing." For example, "Diving is fun." Dive is a verb; diving, here, is a noun.

A *participle* is an adjective derived from a verb form of a word and usually ending in "-ing" if it's active—such as, "A burning wick"—or "-ed" if it's passive—for instance, "Confused, they got lost."

There. Figuring out whether something is a gerund or participle is as easy as falling off a log. Which brings us to another source of confusion . . .

Simile/Metaphor

It's like this.

A *metaphor* is a comparison implied by the juxtaposition of words *without* using "like" or "as"—for instance, "He's an elephant when he dances," or, "His mind's an encyclopedia."

A *simile* is an explicit comparison of two distinctly different things *using* the words "like" or "as." For instance, "His explanation was as clear as an unmuddied lake," or, "He shuns the sun like a vampire."

Mind you, educators consider "like" to be highly idiomatic when used in similes like—that is, *as*—these. However, while "like" is colloquial, it makes some phrases less clunky—for instance, "He ran like mad." If you were to say, "He ran as mad," you'd be regarded as a pompous boor . . . like it or not!

Argot/Dialect/Jargon/Lingo

A rose by any other name may smell as sweet, but would you really have wanted to smell one if you were a soldier during World War I, when a Rose or Rosalie was a bayonet? Probably not. And remember when fusion was something associated with physics and not jazz/pop music?

Despite the opposition of many educators, colloquial language has proliferated in the United States and elsewhere—especially in recent years, when it is politically incorrect to dis colloquialisms that are closely identified with different ethnic groups.

Variations in the language are divided into the following groupings.

Argot is the vocabulary unique to a class or group of people, meant to be understood only by them for private communication—such as "mop" (hobo talk for "the railroad") or "gat" (underworldese for "any firearm").

Dialect is language distinguished from other varieties of the same language by features such as grammar and vocabulary. It usually evolves among a group of speakers who are set off from the others geographically. A Brooklynite's "dese" for "these" is dialect. Dialectal words have the same meaning as their nondialectal counterparts.

Jargon (or *lexicon*) is the language or vocabulary of a particular trade, profession, or group—for example, words used by attorneys, CIA operatives, and others. As opposed to argot and dialect, jargon is usually considered to be an "educated" kind of language.

Lingo is strange or foreign speech. Chinese may be standard to someone from China, but it's viewed as lingo when it's heard by an ordinary citizen outside the country of China. The term "lingo" is generally used disparagingly.

Malapropism/Spoonerism

Though idiosyncratic language is at least tolerated in many circles, out-and-out gaffes such as these are not.

In 1775, Richard Sheridan wrote *The Rivals*, a comedy in which Mrs. Malaprop (a name inspired by the French expression *mal à propos*, or "badly suited") misapplied words, such as, "As headstrong as an allegory on the banks of the Nile." Today, a *malapropism* describes any inappropriate usage when one of the words sounds nearly correct but isn't, such as, "Lead the way and we'll precede." Comedian Norm Crosby built a career around malapropisms.

In real life, the English clergyman W. A. Spooner (1844–1930) was famous for his tendency to transpose the first letters or sounds of words, such as, "A blushing crow" instead of "A crushing blow." Today, he is remembered when anyone makes a blunder of that sort, *aka* a *spoonerism*.

Communiqué/Epistle/Letter/Missive

A *letter* is any communication in writing, type, or print, addressed to a person or persons and delivered, rather than read over the telephone or transmitted by any form of facsimile.

A *missive* is a short, usually curt letter that's handwritten. The word comes from *letters missive*, orders from a sovereign carried by messenger to a specific person.

An *epistle* is a formal and often didactic letter, such as one that states church doctrine or a political position.

Any of these can also be a *communiqué*, an informational—albeit usually very short—message.

If you write a large number of letters or epistles, you may decide to collect them in a book. In that case, you'll want to be aware of two very important distinctions. . . .

Print/Publish

The front page of every issue of the *New York Times* trumpets that it has, "All the News That's Fit to Print."

Whether much of the news (and many of the reviews) are fit to publish is another matter; the two are not the same.

To *print* is to cause text or illustrations to be reproduced by mechanical means, through the transfer of ink or dyes, to another surface.

To *publish* is to distribute printed material to the public. Even if the work is impounded or warehoused for some reason—for example, by a strike—the intent to distribute renders it "published."

Obviously, books and newspapers are published, but what about flyers handed out on street corners? If they're photocopied or run off on a computer, the answer is *maybe*. Though electronics and computer technology are widely used in publishing, mimeographed or electronic reproduction on paper is defined as *duplication*, not publication, as it has gone through a copying process and nothing more. However, legal case histories hold distributors of flyers liable for libel, and the courts may have something there. As the Roman poet Persius said in the first century A.D., "*In nihilum nil posse reverti*: Anything once produced cannot become nothing again."

Book/Volume/Tome

What you're reading now, of course, has been published. It's a *book*, consecutive sheets of paper bound between two covers. These particular covers happen to be soft, but a book can have hard or soft covers, the pages can be bound together by thread, glue, or spiral rings, the subject can be any kind of fiction or nonfiction, and the dimensions of the finished product can be long, squat, narrow, thin, small, or thick.

A book may be a *volume*, but more often than not that word implies one book in a series, such as the "A" volume of an encyclopedia, the first volume of a trilogy, one volume of Edward Gibbon's *The History of the Decline and Fall of the Roman Empire*, etc.

A *tome* is also a book, but one that is either very heavy, physically, or whose contents are heavy intellectually. *The Oxford English Dictionary* is the former; works such as *Moby Dick* and *Ben-Hur* are the latter. (Well, actually, you *can* get quite a workout toting around a hardbound Melville or Wallace.)

Anthology/Compendium

Suppose you were to publish a tome full of those letters of yours we were discussing earlier. Would that be considered an anthology or a compendium?

If you have a thick book of any short pieces, be they poems, stories, prayers, songs, etc., it's an *anthology*. Anthologies can be a collection of writings by either various authors or by a single author. Your book of letters or a collection of *Aesop's Fables* would be an anthology.

If you're cramming a great many works into a relatively small space, the book is called a *compendium*. Material in a compendium is usually condensed or summarized—for example, movie plots, medical information, etc. An almanac is considered a compendium.

Annals/Chronicles

How do we know what happened in 1960, or in 1060, for that matter? We get our information from historical records, which often take the form of annals or chronicles.

Annals are a yearly record of events or achievements (hence the name, from the Latin root *annus* for "year") told in chronological order.

Chronicles (from the Greek root *chrono-*, for "time") describe a record of any lengthy historical event, such as a war or reign, both of which tend to last for years.

Sadly, not all peoples kept records over the years, which is why information on historical events can often be so skimpy.

Aphorism/Apothegm/Idiom/
Maxim/Motto/Proverb/Saw

One very popular kind of anthology is a collection of wise and/or witty quotations. But "There's more than one way to skin a cat," and there's more than one way to express a universal truth in twenty-five words or less. It all depends on the tone you want to convey.

An *aphorism* is a short, pithy, instructive saying, such as the one above.

A *maxim* is a self-righteous or moralistic aphorism; for example, "Man is the measure of all things."

An *apothegm* is an edgy, often cynical aphorism, such as, "Men are generally more careful of the breed of their horses and dogs than of their children."

An *idiom* is an expression whose meaning can't be derived simply by hearing it, such as "Kick the bucket."

A *motto* is an expression that embodies the philosophy of a person or group, such as, "People are our most important business."

A *proverb*—which is synonymous with an *adage*—is a short, popular saying that expresses a truth or insight; for example, "A word to the wise is sufficient."

A *saw* is an extremely quaint proverb, such as, "You can lead a horse to water, but you can't make him drink."

And as they say, "That's it in a nutshell."

Legend/Myth/Tall Tale

A *legend* is story that has grown up around an event or figure that usually has some historical basis. Legends are typically an oral tradition, handed down from generation to generation, with apocryphal elements frequently added in the retelling—for example, the idea that Davy Crockett "kilt him a b'ar" when he was three years old.

A *myth* is a legend about ancient gods, demigods, and mortals, a tale that belongs to and very much typifies a particular culture. Like legends, myths are fiction, though many of them also involve historical figures.

A *tall tale* is a form of storytelling, popularized in America, in which the origins of natural phenomena are given fantastic explanations, such as Paul Bunyan inadvertently creating the Mississippi River when his water tank burst, or Pecos Bill digging a trench, filling it with water from the Gulf of Mexico, and creating the Rio Grande. Of the three types of stories, tall tales have the skimpiest moral content . . . yet because they're so outrageous, they're often the most fun!

All three narrative forms exist because most storytellers fix their imagination to a long leash—most, but not all.

Journalist/Reporter

For some people, fact is more important than fiction. In "A Dream," Robert Burns wrote, "But Facts are chiels that winna ding, an' downa be disputed." Meaning? Don't dispute them. In Charles Dickens's *Hard Times*, Mr. Gradgrind uttered, "Facts alone are wanted in life." (An odd thing indeed for a fictitious character to say . . .)

Among writers, reporters, and journalists are the ones who concern themselves with facts, although in different ways and often to different degrees.

A *reporter* is someone who gathers or digs up news and/or facts and usually writes up the copy about them in an objective fashion, most often for a newspaper or regularly scheduled broadcast.

A *journalist* can be that, but is also anyone who edits, photographs, publishes, or transmits the news *or* topics of interest for any of the media, including magazines and books. However, a journalist can also write subjectively: columnists, critics, and editorial writers all infuse their work with their own point of view.

By definition, the terms "photojournalist" and "investigative reporter" are redundant.

Critique/Review

Critics, as we've said, are also journalists, though as the saying goes, "Those who can't do, teach, and those who can't teach become critics."

Actually, that isn't *quite* right. There are two forms of criticism, one of them constructive and usually unbiased and written for the creator, the other often destructive and idiosyncratic and written for the consumer.

The former is a *critique*, an article or report, printed or spoken, which evaluates a work, usually while it's still a work in progress. A critique frequently includes suggestions for improvement, and is often tendered by a respected colleague.

The less helpful kind of evaluation is a *review*, an article or report that rates the finished product, be it a play, book, movie, automobile, VCR, or computer. The reviewer is presumably (but not always!) qualified in the area he/she is reviewing, and, unlike a critique, a review is designed to inform *and* entertain the reader or listener—often at the subject's expense.

Having said that, the worse reviewer on the planet is still preferable to someone whose job is to . . .

Censor/Expurgate

In Imperial Rome, a censor was someone charged with, among other duties, supervising public manners and morality. If the censor deemed someone to be immoral, he had the authority to cause a mark of some kind to be made on the offender; for example, a sign could be hung around them detailing their crime, etc.

Today, symbolically, we're still putting scarlet letters on people via negative publicity generated by causing offense to some segment of the population. As a result, expurgation has replaced censorship as the bane of the arts.

To *censor* is to delete material prior to its being issued, based on what someone (usually a person or board guided by very conservative criteria) feels will be objectionable on moral or political grounds.

Expurgate is to remove offensive or objectionable material after something has been published, screened, displayed, etc., in response to an outcry from a segment of the public.

Anyone who practices either deserves to be *censured*—disapproved of, usually in public and always in the most emphatic terms.

FANTASY

Giant/Titan

In 1960, there already was an NFL team called the New York Giants, so the new AFL franchise called their new team the New York Titans (now the Jets). Could the Giants have sued for unfair competition?

No. The two fantastic beings are completely different.

Giants are beings who are bigger than people. According to Greek mythology, they were created when the blood of the wounded god Uranus struck the earth. Norse tales give them various monstrous forms and describe them being so large as to create winds and storms simply by the flapping of their wings, while giants in Celtic mythology are said to have torn rocks from the mainland to create islands in the sea. In American folklore, the giant Paul Bunyan was twenty feet long by the time he was a month old.

Titans are beings who are larger than giants. The offspring of the god Uranus and the goddess Gaea, there were originally just twelve of them; later, the term was broadened to include the huge offspring of the Titans as well (such as Atlas). Today, the term is used to describe any big, unstoppable force.

Meanwhile, at the other end of the size spectrum . . .

Elves/Fairies/Leprechauns/Pixies

Size isn't everything. Though giants and titans are powerful beings, they tend to be fairly benign. Traditionally, it's the little people who cause the most trouble.

Elves, a product of Scandinavian lore, are little people who possess magical powers. Their home is Elfheim and they're subjects of the Elf King, who sends them off into the woods to work mischief on travelers.

Fairies are a more diverse lot. They originated in ancient Europe, where they were thought to be the spirits of the dead, who, because of some minor infraction during their lifetime, hadn't made the grade to angel. Depending upon the culture, fairies can be the size of a bird or fully human in stature, and either they're good, devoted to helping humans, or quite evil, dedicated to humankind's destruction.

Leprechauns are Irish shoemaker fairies, old men standing two feet tall and living in quiet places such as woods and wine cellars. They wear a cocked hat, lace coat, knee breeches, and shoes with silver buckles. While they live in out-of-the-way places, they are extremely wealthy—a virtue of charging a great deal for their wares and living to a ripe old age. Though they are malicious when they're drunk, when sober they can be persuaded to give money to needy people. The word "leprechaun" comes from *leith bhrogan,* "one shoe maker," underscoring their diligence as they completely finish one shoe before moving on to another.

Pixies are the souls of those who have never been baptized, including non-Christians, newborns, and people who died before the coming of Jesus. Like elves, they delight in teasing travelers; like fairies, they come in many different sizes.

Gnome/Gremlin/Troll

Sometimes included with fairies, sometimes with giants, these fantastic creatures are often confused with one another.

In medieval times, *gnomes* were one of the four Elementals, creatures that looked after the four elements (*sylphs* tended to the air, *Nereids* the waters, *salamanders* [see entry, page 154] fire, and *gnomes* the earth). Gnomes could move freely through the soil—and, so doing, often discovered gems, precious metals, and other treasures. In time, they became miners, and greedy ones at that, short, shriveled, pale old men who were fond of playing tricks on humans who came seeking their treasure. The word comes from the Greek *gnōmē*, or "intelligence," since these little men possessed knowledge of hidden wealth.

Originally symbols of fertility, *trolls* are Scandinavian beings, giants that guarded great treasure. When the ancient pagan religions became myths, trolls became a part of folklore, this time as mischievous, redheaded hunchbacks nearly as tall as a human. Usually dressed in dark clothes and a red cap, they delighted in their favorite pastimes: dancing and stealing babies. The word "troll" derives from the Scandinavian word for "giant."

Gremlins are a creation of the aeronautic era and gained prominence during World War II. Whenever something inexplicable went wrong with the electrical or mechanical elements in an aircraft, aviators blamed a gremlin, a combination bulldog and jackrabbit that wore breeches, a red jacket, spats, and a top hat, had ducklike feet, and lived in ditches and holes near the airfields. Since the end of the war, gremlins have been said to plague all kinds of electrical or mechanical systems. The word derives from the obsolete word "greme" (to vex) with the suffix "-lin," from "goblin."

Apparition/Ghost/Poltergeist/Specter

"From ghoulies and ghosties and long-leggety
    beasties
And things that go bump in the night,
    Good Lord, deliver us!

Those anonymous lines were written hundreds of years ago in Cornwall, a land known for its giants, not its ghosts. Or poltergeists. Or apparitions. Or specters.

These creatures exist in every corner of the world; even in our own culture, they come in many different shades.

A *ghost* is a disembodied spirit, the invisible or translucent soul of a dead person wandering in our plane of existence. Spiritualists tell us that ghosts are comprised of an invisible bodily substance called ectoplasm, which wafts from the pores upon death and can hover in the air or enter the body of another or an inanimate object.

When ectoplasm is visible, the ghost is called an *apparition*.

When an apparition does more than just hang in the air—when it wails or pursues an observer or acts in an aggressive or terrifying manner—it's known as a *specter*.

When a ghost actually possesses or handles nonliving matter, pushing it around a room or rapping on walls, tables, ceilings, etc., that ghost is called a *poltergeist*. Poltergeists are ghosts that are either mischievous or simply can't accept the fact that they're dead and take so their frustration out on the living.

Other nonspecific terms used interchangeably with ghosts are *phantom*, *spook*, *phantasm*, *wraith*, and *shade*.

Flying Saucer/UFO

On June 24, 1947, pilot Kenneth Arnold saw nine disklike objects flying over the skies of Washington and described them as saucers. A reporter covering the story coined the term *flying saucer*, and since that time it's been used to describe any flattened, oval object presumed to have come from another planet.

But through the years—as far back as Columbus's crossing of the Atlantic—people have been seeing strange flying objects, from cigar-shaped to globelike, and in many sizes. Since these objects definitely were not saucers, the term *UFO* or Unidentified Flying Object was coined (when and by whom is unknown), legitimized by the Air Force in Project Bluebook, which from 1948 to 1969 catalogued 13,000 UFO sightings.

The misconception about UFOs is that they are alien spaceships. In fact, they are simply any object that can't be identified at the time. When they're shown to have been weather balloons, low-flying aircraft, marsh gas, etc., they are referred to as IFOs (Identified Flying Objects). Interestingly, some researchers hold that UFOs are not spaceships at all, but terrestrial time travelers.

ART AND PHOTOGRAPHY

Chroma/Color/Hue/Shade/Tinge/Tint/Tone

This isn't the math and science section, but let's get physics-al for just a second, shall we?

All objects absorb or reflect light, and every color is present in light, each with its own particular wavelength. The color of an object is determined by the wavelength(s) the object fails to absorb, the color of these wavelength(s) bouncing back to our eyes as fast as bullets rebounding off of Superman's chest.

If just one wavelength comes back pure (either red, orange, yellow, green, blue, indigo, or violet), the reflected light is referred to as the *color* of the object. Black (no wavelengths returning) and white (all wavelengths returning) are also considered colors.

If there's a combination of colors, however slight, the reflected light is known as the *hue* of the object.

The *shade* of a color is the level of its lightness or darkness; navy blue as opposed to sky blue, for example.

The amount of white present in a color determines its *tint*; conversely, the amount of color present in white is known as a *tinge*.

The *chroma* of a color is its combined level of purity (its freedom from tint) and intensity (its brightness), which together are known as "saturation": a red that's twenty percent saturated will have a washed-out chroma compared to one that's eighty percent saturated.

The combination of chroma and shade describes the *tone* of a color.

Hope we've shed some light on the subject.

Carmine/Cherry/Crimson/Magenta/Maroon/ Red/Ruby/Scarlet/Vermilion

If the first Sherlock Holmes story had been titled *A Study in Cherry* instead of *A Study in Scarlet*, would the Baker Street detective have attracted the interest he did? Or if Robert Burns had written, "O my luve's like a ruby, ruby rose," would the line have endured any better than the meter?

Probably not in both cases. There's something to be said for selecting the right word for the right job, even if the meaning is identical or similar.

But just how similar *are* the different forms of red? There's a surprisingly wide range sandwiched between orange and purple.

Upon leaving *red*, which is one of the three primary colors (yellow and blue being the others) and heading toward orange, we find *cherry* (or carnelian), a bright red; *scarlet*, a brighter red; and *vermilion*, a bright scarlet.

On the opposite side of the scale, there's *ruby* (or cerise), a deep red; *carmine*, a mild purplish red; *crimson*, a deep carmine; *magenta*, which is a reddish purple; and *maroon*, a brownish red. Other variations, such as bloodred, flame-red, and lobster-red, are all informal names for or combinations of the above.

Fresco/Mural

When Leonardo da Vinci rendered his magnificent *The Last Supper* in Milan, he did so with oil paints on a damp wall. That proved to be a mistake, for the oil and moisture didn't mix, and the paint began to peel not long after Leonardo's death. He had created a mural, but erred when he failed to make it a fresco.

A *mural* is artwork that's executed on a wall and occasionally, by extension, on a ceiling. It can also be done elsewhere, and then permanently affixed to a wall.

A *fresco* also can be that, but it must meet certain criteria: it has to be painted on a damp, plaster surface, and it must be rendered with watercolors that will become one with the dried plaster.

Michelangelo used the fresco technique to paint the ceiling and walls of the Sistine Chapel, and the work has survived over four centuries of waxy candle smoke, pollution, and botched restoration.

Engraving/Etching/Lithograph/Woodcut

One thing you can do that neither Leonardo nor Michelangelo did is invite someone to your apartment to see your etchings. Unfortunately, when your guest arrives, you find out, much to your embarrassment, that what you've got aren't etchings but engravings. Your guest departs, leaving you to wonder just where you went wrong. For future reference:

An *engraving* is made by using a cutting tool to scratch a design on the surface of a metal plate, block of wood, or the like, and from it ink impressions or prints are made.

An *etching* is a design carved into wax atop a metal or glass plate. A corrosive substance such as acid is poured on that and burns the exposed design into the plate, which is then used to create copies on paper.

Both of these art forms are known as "intaglio printing," printing from designs cut into a surface. *Woodcuts* or *linocuts* are different: they're "relief printing," where the artist gouges the wood or linoleum block and creates a design in the raised area.

A *lithograph* is flat or "planographic printing," a print taken from an image on a stone or metal (usually zinc) plate. The design is rendered with a greasy crayon or paint, which is coated with water, then ink. The grease repels the water but not the ink, while the water prevents the ink from adhering to the rest of the block. As a result, when paper is pressed on top of the stone, only the design is printed. A different coat of ink must be used for each color, which makes the process quite time consuming.

Daguerreotype/Photographic Film/Tintype

Photographic film was invented in 1877 by Hannibal Williston Goodwin, who received a patent for his "nitro cellulose transparent flexible photographic film pellicles." Roll film for cameras was patented by David Henderson Houston four years later, and in 1884 George Eastman contributed the modern transparent strip film coated with a gelatin emulsion.

Before that, photographs were taken on stiff surfaces that required exposures of fifteen minutes to an hour to soak up enough light to produce an image. What's more, these were positive images: there were no negatives from which duplicates could be produced.

The *tintype (aka ferrotype)* is the oldest form of photography, invented in 1826 by Joseph Nicephore Niepce. The surface of the picture was enameled tin or iron, which had been coated with iodine. After the plate was exposed, the image was brought out using mercury vapor.

The *daguerreotype* was another early form of photograph, invented in 1837 by Niepce's partner L.J.M. Daguerre. Daguerreotypes were taken on a silvered glass or metal surface and were less cumbersome than tintypes.

Get the picture?!

Collage/Montage

There's an old art school joke about putting together presidential campaign buttons, ribbons, and photographs on a board and creating an electoral collage. The pun may be weak, but the definition is on the money.

A *collage* is a work of art in which, on a single surface, the artist has fixed images and/or materials not usually associated with one another (the electoral collage being the latter).

A *montage* is a photographic or cinematographic work in which elements from various sources, but of a similar kind, are juxtaposed, superimposed, or otherwise combined. In other words, it can't consist of materials that are different physically, only ones that are different visually.

A photomontage can be described as a collage, though

only in the sense that the images are not usually associated with one another.

And what do artists use to make many of their collages and montages? Some use hot wax, which fixes the image in place when it dries. Others use . . .

Glue/Paste

Why do folks always joke about sending an old horse to the glue factory, but never to the paste factory?

Because before the advent of ingredients like methyl-ethyl-ketone and petroleum distillates, *glue* was made from protein gelatin, which, when the skin, hoofs, and other parts of animals were boiled in water, separated out and sunk to the bottom of the water.

Paste, on the other hand, has always been a mixture of water, flour, and starch in various proportions. Paste is less adhesive, but is also less macabre and easier on the stomach than glue.

MUSIC

Concertmaster/Conductor/Maestro

The word "music" comes from the Greek *mousikē*, the art of the muse. Where orchestras are concerned, there is more than one muse: the composer who creates the score, and the person who brings it to life. The musician is there to carry out the vision of the latter.

A *conductor* is the person who directs an orchestra and/or chorus. He or she interprets the music, perhaps emphasizing different instruments or experimenting with the tempo in rehearsals, then leading the musicians or singers in the performance.

A *concertmaster* is the assistant to the conductor of a symphony orchestra, and is usually the leader of the first violins. This tradition stems from the fact that until the middle nineteenth century, conductors tended to direct performances using a violin bow; they eventually changed to sticks, so they could beat the time audibly.

Either one of these two people can be considered a *maestro*—that is, an eminent composer, conductor, musician, or teacher of music.

Octave/Scale

Playing a scale and playing *for* scale are different matters.

A *scale* is a series of eight notes played in alphabetical order, ascending or descending according to fixed intervals. These notes can be naturals (the white keys on a piano), sharps, or flats (the black keys). The series begins on the keynote, after which the scale is named (for example, C or

F-sharp), and always ends on that same note an octave higher.

An *octave* is the *distance* covered by the eight notes of any scale. In other words, it's the *span* between a note and the next higher or lower note that has the same name. The range of any instrument or voice is indicated by the number of octaves it encompasses.

Refrain/Repeat

Suppose you suddenly lose your mind and decide to do some *karaoke* singing. You're up there on the stage, ripping through some Beatles tunes, when all of a sudden you're faced with the words, "Ob-la-di, ob-la-da."

Are you singing a refrain, or is it a repeat?

It's a *refrain*, also known as the chorus, a part of the music—involving notes and/or words—that recurs several times during the course of the piece.

A *repeat* is a section of music that the composer wants you to play once again at a certain point, after which you continue through the piece. A repeat is indicated on a sheet of music by a double bar line with two dots on the side.

After your *karaoke* performance, you decide you simply *must* chuck your present career and pursue a life of music. But you realize that being able to tell a refrain from a repeat isn't enough. For example, you've also got to know the difference between . . .

Air/Aria/Ballad/Ditty/Jingle/ Melody/Song/Tune

A *song* is a metrical composition meant to be sung, with at least four rhymed stanzas (each of which is usually a group of four lines). A song tells a story or expresses a sentiment or idea, and often contains two separate melodies (one, then another, then a repeat of the first).

A *ballad* is a romantic song that uses the same melody for each stanza.

A *ditty* is a short, simple song that tells a story.

A *jingle* is shorter than a song, with uncomplicated sounds or passages that are presented and then repeated, often more than once. A jingle expresses an idea or feeling, but does not tell a story.

A *melody* and a *tune* are the same thing, a sequence of notes that produce a rhythmic whole. A melody may make up one part of a song, although lyrics are not a part of a melody, nor is harmony.

An *air* is the main melody in a harmonized composition, especially the soprano or treble part; an air can be performed on its own.

An *aria* is an ornate sing-alone air with musical accompaniment, which is usually part of an opera or oratorio. Which brings us to . . .

Comic Opera/Grand Opera/Opera/Operetta

An *opera* is a tale that's acted out onstage to the accompaniment of music and has all its dialogue sung—usually with a range and complexity that would send most singers packing. There are many different kinds of operas, the major ones being:

Comic opera is an opera that has humor, a buffoon or two, and a story that, while often complex, is never downbeat. Comic operas often have a number of passages that are spoken rather than sung, such as Mozart's *The Magic Flute.*

Grand opera is just the opposite: an opera with a depressing or tragic subject, usually performed on a huge scale with magnificent costumes and great sets. Borodin's *Prince Igor* and Verdi's *Aida* are examples of grand opera at its grandest.

None of these types of operas have dancing, per se, which is where the *operetta* (or *light opera*) comes in. The forerunner of the modern-day musical, *operettas* have light, fun stories similar to comic operas, although there is a good deal more spoken dialogue and the songs are often accompanied by dancing. The works of Gilbert and Sullivan (*The Pirates of Penzance*) and Victor Herbert (*Babes in Toyland*) are operettas.

Dixieland/Jazz/Ragtime

At the opposite end of the musical spectrum from strictly structured opera is *jazz*, an American musical form that originated among black musicians around the turn of the century in New Orleans.

The hallmarks of jazz are ensemble improvisation (though jazz today is often arranged), driving rhythms, dissonances, melodic variations, distinctive tonal effects on horns and reed instruments, and music based on a wide range of scales, including diatonic (five whole notes and two semitones) and chromatic (semitones only). The word "jazz" may have come from the French verb *jaser*, to talk indiscreetly, although many etymologists claim that this sexually charged music came from *jism*, a slang term for male ejaculate.

Dixieland is hard-driving jazz, the pure New Orleans improvisational music in strongly accented four-four time with virtuoso solos.

Ragtime is a slightly older musical form, having originated some ten years before the turn of the century. It's usually played on the piano, and is typified by a two-four "march" time beat and a melody that has room for improvisation. The term derives from the form's "ragged" or syncopated time—that is, the stressing of normally unaccented beats.

Minstrel/Troubadour

Early in the Middle Ages, long before even opera had emerged as a musical form, songs, ballads, and even ditties were being popularized in the Middle Ages by *minstrels* (or balladeers), men who roamed the countryside, singing or reciting poetry in town squares, at fairs, or in the courts, and accompanying themselves on stringed instruments. These men wrote their own music or carried music they had heard from town to town; some were even skillful enough to create ditties on demand.

In nineteenth- and early twentieth-century America, a *minstrel* was a white man who worked in a minstrel troupe, made himself up in blackface, and sang songs, told jokes, and performed skits in theaters.

A *troubadour* was also a medieval minstrel, but one who sang compositions that had a complex metrical form and were written in the langue d'oc, the Romance language of Southern France (which is where troubadours originated and for the most part plied their trade from the eleventh through the thirteenth centuries). These men usually accompanied themselves on early forms of the guitar called bandurrias or citterns, which were also forerunners of the mandolin and other stringed instruments.

Banjo/Mandolin/Ukulele

You know what a guitar is because you played one during the "Clapton is God" years, or around the campfire, or in college when you should have been studying. But when it comes to other plectrum-plucked instruments, you aren't sure you could tell them apart. Well, fret no more!

A *banjo* is a musical instrument of the guitar family. It has either four or five strings pulled over a circular body whose front is tightly stretched skin or parchment. The instrument takes its name from the *bandore*, an obsolete stringed instrument based on the ancient Roman pandūra and a medieval teardrop-shaped bandurria.

A *mandolin* has a wooden, pear-shaped body with a deep sound box, a fretted neck, and either eight, ten, or twelve metal strings. The mandolin also derives its name from the pandūra (although no one knows how or why the first letter was changed).

A *ukulele* is a four-stringed instrument that resembles a small guitar. It originated in Hawaii and takes its name from *uku*, "insect," and *lele* "jumps," which describes the player's finger movements.

Fiddle/Violin

Did Nero really fiddle while Rome burned? If so, he wasn't playing a fiddle as we know it. That instrument didn't come into existence until the seventeenth century, long after the first century A.D. emperor was dead.

If Nero made music, he did so on a lyre or kithara, which were forerunners of the harp and guitar, respectively.

The *violin*—like its increasingly larger cousins the viola, cello, and bass viol—is a four-stringed instrument, more or less hourglass-shaped and played with a bow. There are distinctive S or C-shaped sound holes in the soundboard, and an elegant scroll at the top of the pegbox. Violins are prominent instruments in orchestras.

Fiddle comes from the Latin *vitulari*, "to rejoice," and is a colloquial word used to describe a violin that's played in folk music. The instrument is the same as a "normal" violin, except in Greece and the Balkans, where it describes a specific three-stringed folk instrument. However, as players tend to tap a foot and swing the bow arm in time with the music, "to fiddle" is often used disparagingly to describe playing that isn't very serious.

Fife/Flute/Piccolo

While jokers talk about violinists fiddling around, there's also an old vaudeville gag about a troupe of flautists that was so bad they took their instruments and blew away.

A *flute* is any wind instrument consisting of a tube with six or more finger holes (or "keys") in which the player's breath is directed against a sharp edge (i. e., the flute is held transversely, out to the side) or through a flue (as in a recorder).

A *piccolo* is a small flute that plays notes that lie an octave higher than a flute. A *fife* is also a small high-pitched flute, but is slightly larger and a tone lower than the piccolo. Fifes may have anywhere from one to six keys, and are played almost exclusively in fife-and-drum bands.

Clavichord/Harpsichord/Piano/Spinet

When Frédéric Chopin was a little boy, did his parents yell at him to practice the *piano*? Or in 1816, which is when he took his first lessons, was he playing some other clavier (a keyboard instrument)?

No, it was a piano—which, by then, was pretty much the instrument we know today. It evolved from a series of keyboard instruments, the oldest of which was the *harpsichord*, invented some time in the fourteenth century. Horizontal or trapezoid shaped, the harpsichord had a series of taut strings that were plucked by quills or leather fingers attached to the keys.

By the seventeenth century, harpsichords boasted two and sometimes three keyboards, one atop the other, which allowed the player a greater range, or, simply, the ability to produce different sounds.

Harpsichords with one keyboard were called *spinets*, a term that replaced *virginals*, so-called because they were played by young girls.

The *clavichord* evolved from the harpsichord. Developed early in the fifteenth century, it was an oblong instrument that consisted of strings arranged parallel to the keyboard that were struck (rather than plucked) by small brass blades, a development important to the creation of the modern-day piano.

The *piano*—or, more correctly, the *pianoforte*—grew from the clavichord and produces sounds by a combination of keyboard-driven hammers striking strings, with dampers and pedals used to create different tones. The first pianos were produced in 1710; the space-saving upright piano was perfected in 1800.

The different sized pianos—*baby grand*, *grand*, and *concert grand*—were created to generate a sound that had the proper tone and body for halls of different sizes.

Pianolas, or player pianos, were introduced late in the eighteenth century and played by means of rotating paper rolls whose slits corresponded to the note to be played, and its duration. The rolls were typically placed in cabinets inset in the front of the instrument, directly above the keyboard.

Accordion/Concertina

Sometimes, it just isn't practical to cart a piano around with you. For that reason, in 1822, German inventor

Friedrich Buschmann came up with a Slinkylike instrument called the *accordion*, also known as a "squeeze box." Although still quite a handful, the instrument consisted of a large fabric or paper bellows with a keyboard on one side and buttons on the other (for playing single bass notes or chords, since obviously both hands couldn't be on the same side). The accordion took its name from "accord," i.e., "harmony," which is what the instrument provides a singer (along with powerful arm and wrist muscles!).

Yet, not everyone could afford or carry an accordion, so in 1829 Sir Charles Wheatstone came up with the bright idea of creating a smaller version: a hexagonal instrument with bellows, hard ends, a strap for the hand on one side, and buttonlike keys on the other. The result was an instrument of limited range but high portability: the *concertina*, used for giving a little concert.

Of course, the idea of people getting their music from a street corner or even a concert hall is becoming more and more passé in these days of digital, surround-sound home audio and video systems. Which brings us to our final musical entry ...

Tweeter/Woofer

Remember the first time you heard these words and you thought someone was pulling your leg? How could anyone talk seriously about *tweeters*, for goodness sake? And *woofers*.

But there's a reason these elements in audio speakers are called what they are. In fact, the distinction is rather self-explanatory.

Tweeters are components that bring out the high-frequency sounds, and they're named in honor of the high-frequency sounds made by birds.

Woofers bring out the low-frequency sounds, and, of course, are named after the barking of dogs.

Subwoofers are speakers that magnify low-frequency sounds into palpable vibrations, turning drumbeats into earthquakes.

MOTION PICTURES

Film/Movie

If you look in most dictionaries, these two words seem to be synonymous: they're both motion pictures. In common usage, however, the words have different meanings.

A *movie* is a motion picture whose primary purpose is to entertain. It may do so grandly, such as a James Bond adventure, it may be animated, or it may be a slapstick comedy. It may be made with sublime technical artistry, such as *Gone with the Wind*, or it may be a cheap horror film. If it's fun, even sophisticated fun, it's a movie.

A *film* is a motion picture whose director feels that he or she has something important to say. A film may be enjoyable—*Citizen Kane* is certainly that—but its reason for being is to enlighten its audience, to take a serious look at some subject, or, at the very least, showcase a filmmaker's vision (or pretention).

Many filmmakers tend to look down their noses at moviemakers, but chances are good folks will still be watching the movies of Cecil B. DeMille when the works of today's hot "geniuses" are collecting dust on video store shelves.

Score/Soundtrack

A *score* is the music composed for a motion picture or TV series, while a *soundtrack* is the recorded music actually used in a movie or TV show (although when moviemakers, not composers, use the term "soundtrack," they mean *every* sound in the film, from the music, to the voices, to the extraneous noises).

Those distinctions are easy enough, though things change when the music is marketed for consumers.

A commercially sold "original soundtrack" *should* be the actual recording used in the film and transferred from the movie to the CD or tape; occasionally, it is. More often than not, though, it's the same music rerecorded, which may not be exactly what was heard in the film. In the re-recording process, composers often indulge themselves, performing the music in a way that suits them musically rather than simply re-creating what worked best for the film.

(Soundtrack releases from musical films like *West Side Story* or *Grease* are always from the actual movie soundtrack, however, as it's prohibitively expensive to bring the musicians *and* singers or movie stars back to the studio for new sessions.)

But rerecordings are not the only thing of which consumers should be aware.

Until the 1980s, if a recording said "the original score," that meant instrumental music with, perhaps, a sung theme song. With the release of films like *Batman* and *Dick Tracy*, where there were songs sung by rock singers *and* instrumental music, multiple albums were released, with "original score" meaning only instrumental music and "original soundtrack" meaning only vocal music.

That's the score on scores! And if you think *that's* convoluted . . .

CinemaScope/Cinerama/Panavision

Back in the late 1940s and early 1950s, Hollywood feared that television was going to kill the movies: why, they reasoned, would people pay to go out and see what they could get for free at home? (So why did Hollywood go on to sell their old movies to TV? They also reasoned, if you can't beat 'em . . .)

As a way of countering the perceived threat, film studios came up with ways of making movies bigger than ever—literally. Until the early 1950s, the ratio of most screen images was 1.33:1—roughly the same shape as a modern-day TV. (Which is why, when you watch old movies on TV, you don't lose any of the image on the sides.)

However, beginning with Cinerama in 1952 and CinemaScope in 1953, films were shot in different "aspect ratios." Movies made in Cinerama were 3:1 (three times as long as they were tall), while CinemaScope films were 2.35:1

Cinerama was a process in which the film was shot with three separate cameras and projected by three synchronized projectors onto a wide, curved screen. It wasn't until 1963 that technicians came up with a way of filling the same screen with a single, seamless picture (actually a form of Panavision known as Super or Ultra Panavision). The last Cinerama film was made in 1970.

CinemaScope is an anamorphic or "squeezed" film process. In order to show wide-screen pictures in theaters without reequipping them for Cinerama, Hollywood simply compressed images onto "normal-sized" film; these were then unsqueezed in theaters by using existing projectors equipped with a single, special lens. CinemaScope is a trademark of Twentieth Century Fox; other studios had similar processes, such as Technirama and WarnerScope. All of these were discontinued in the late 1960s as screens shrunk in size and owners preferred . . .

Panavision, an anamorphic process that offers a less severe series of aspect ratios, the most common being 1.66:1 and 1.85:1.

(In order to show wide-screen movies on TV, they are usually "panned and scanned." That is, when the films are transferred to video, the technician covers only that section of the image that he/she feels is important. Obviously, that destroys the director's compositions and eliminates one character or another when they're speaking from the opposite side of the screen. Today, many directors shoot their films "TV-safe," centering the action in a 1.33:1 area.)

Double/Stand-In/Understudy

Actors may very well be overpaid for the work they do, but you may be surprised to find that they don't even do all the work that's attributed to them! For instance:

A *double* is someone who replaces a featured actor at certain points during production—for example, in a crowd scene or long shot, when the actor won't be identifiable. These "second unit" scenes are usually shot while the main action featuring the star is being filmed elsewhere (or if the star is drunk or incapacitated, as was often the case with Errol Flynn and other high-living actors). A *stunt double* is someone who replaces the actor in a dangerous scene and also is not shown close up.

A *stand-in* is someone who has the same build as the actor and is used when the sets are being lit or scenes are being blocked out (figuring out where the actors and camera should move), etc. This allows the poor, overpaid actor to rest in an opulent trailer or study his/her lines.

An *understudy* is a stage performer who knows a featured player's part and is ready to step in if the actor is ill or being petulant. Understudies usually have minor parts in the play, so they're not being paid just to "hang around."

Bit Part/Cameo/Extra/Walk-On

In any movie there are minor parts of every kind, although some small roles are smaller than others.

An *extra* is an anonymous someone in the background—a pedestrian, a patron in a restaurant, etc., a character with no audible dialogue and no discernible personality.

Someone who has a *walk-on* part is more than an extra—but just barely. Instead of milling around in the background, an actor with a walk-on part is clearly seen, usually doing some distinguishing bit of action—for example, taking an actor's order in a restaurant, delivering a dispatch to a commanding officer, and so on.

A *bit part* is a small role in a film, one in which an actor plays a character with a personality and usually several lines of dialogue.

A *cameo* (almost always, it's unbilled) is when a famous actor does a bit part or walk-on—for instance, Bob Hope and Bing Crosby sitting in the circus grandstand in *The Greatest Show on Earth*, or Charlton Heston appearing as God in *Almost an Angel*.

Advance Showing/Preview/Screening

A big moment in the movie *Singin' in the Rain* occurs when the studio holds a sneak preview of its new film. The results are disastrous, the audience hates it ... but wait! There's still time to fix the movie and turn it into a hit. That's because, in the good old days, previews were a creative process rather than a marketing tool.

A *preview* is a prerelease screening of a film for the public. Although these are still called *sneak previews*, they're anything but. Traditionally, when a sneak preview was held, the title of the film being shown was not revealed until the picture was actually on the screen. That allowed the studio to see how ordinary theatergoers reacted to a film—and not an audience that had come expressly to see this star or that subject. That response enabled the studio to make changes before the movie's general release (for example, reshooting an unsatisfying ending).

Today, the titles of previewing films are announced in ads and changes to content are rarely made after the preview. Moreover, unlike sneak previews, which were often held months before a film's release, a preview today is used to build favorable word-of-mouth a week or so before the film opens.

An *advance showing* is a presentation of the film before it's completely finished. It's usually held for theater owners and potential licensees, so they can determine whether or not they want to hitch their wagon to the film.

A *screening* is simply a showing for critics, typically held a few days before a film is released. Theoretically, this gives critics time to think about the film before writing their review—unlike theater critics, who give their opinions immediately following the premiere.

There's one nice thing about theater critics, though: they give us a chance to segue from movies to ...

THE STAGE AND
LIVE ENTERTAINMENT

Sketch/Skit

Both of these are short theatrical presentations, but their tone is very different.

A *skit* is a short piece of a comical nature, while a *sketch* is a serious playlet that is often improvised. Just how different they are is clear in their roots: sketch—which also applies, of course, to a rough, quick drawing—comes from the Greek *skédios*, or "extempore"; skit is derived from the Icelandic *skītr*, or "excrement"—not necessarily a comment on a skit's artistic merit, but the fact that it's the leavings of a moment.

Black Comedy/Farce/Lampoon/
Parody/Satire/Spoof

One reason comedy is such a broad canvas is because, unlike horror or drama where there are proven formulas and specific buttons to push to get a reaction, everyone responds differently to humor.

Slapstick comedy, from the Keystone Kops to Jerry Lewis to Inspector Clouseau, depends mostly on pratfalls. Intellectual comedy, however, comes in many different forms and works equally well on film, on the stage, or in print.

A *satire* is a humorous work in which human vices, follies, and foibles are held up to ridicule and scorn.

A *lampoon* is a sharper, often mean-spirited satire, while

a *black comedy* is a lampoon whose subject is the opposite of what one would ordinarily consider humorous—death, war, crime, etc.

A *parody* is an imitation of a piece in which fun is poked at the serious tone of the original, while a *spoof* is a parody with a broader, even sillier tone.

In addition to these, there's *farce*, a light, humorous drama, the plot of which depends on a cleverly humorous situation rather than on character development.

Comedian/Comic/Stooge

Except for strippers or women in skimpy costumes doing dances or simply walking across the stage, comedy was the most popular form of entertainment in vaudeville and burlesque. Many great performers got their start on the stage at the turn of the century, among them George Burns, Gracie Allen, Bud Abbott, and Lou Costello.

As we mentioned in the previous entry, comedy embraces a wide variety of styles *and* many different kinds of performers. Chief among these are:

A *comic* (or *stand-up comic*), someone who gets up on the stage and tells (hopefully!) amusing stories or jokes, does funny characters, and uses props if necessary, but doesn't "act," per se—for example, Jay Leno or Shari Lewis.

A *comedian* is someone who may do stand-up comedy, but also performs in funny skits, such as Ernie Kovacs or Steve Martin.

A *stooge* is part of a team, someone who is fed lines by a straight man and/or is the brunt of jokes, by taking pratfalls or pies in the face, etc.

Ad-lib/Extemporize/Improvise

What's the difference between a comedian and a politician? Very little, one might be tempted to say. Yet, there's a difference between them if one or the other has to say something off the cuff.

In giving a speech, a politician or any other person can

extemporize, which is to speak at some length without special preparation and with the help of few, if any, notes. When someone extemporizes, the listener assumes that the speaker has more than a passing familiarity with the subject.

A politician or a performer can also *ad-lib*, which is to speak, act, or perform without any special preparation, but this lasts *very* briefly—for a line or two, at the most.

However, only actors or comedians should *improvise*, which is to act at length without any preparation whatsoever. Politicians who do this are liable to get themselves—and us!—into a world of trouble.

Bon Mot/Gag/Joke/One-Liner/Pun/Riddle

Thought you were through with funny business after only two entries? Not on your life! However, *this* is the kind of entry that makes grown people groan more.

A *joke* is a short story with a twist or pun ending. For instance:

The elderly Mrs. Porter said to her friend, "The doctor told me skipping is a great way to lose weight."

"Skipping? At your age?"

"Sure," Mrs. Porter said. "Skipping lunch, skipping dinner, skipping snacks . . ."

A *gag* is a one- or two-line joke, such as, "There are two letters of the alphabet my dentist loves—*DK*."

A *one-liner* is a funny expression, but one that also illuminates some truth about the world, for example, "The only thing most Broadway actors gain by going to Hollywood is three hours."

A *bon mot* is a one-liner that's usually said at the expense of a person or group, such as, "Fat men have what it takes to attract women: gravity."

A *pun* is a play on words, for instance, "Roller skates are wheely fun."

Usually directed at children, a *riddle* is a question with a silly answer, such as, "What do you call an inch-high zombie? Tomb Thumb."

(See also the entry *Conundrum/Enigma/Puzzle/Riddle*, page 62.)

Legerdemain/Prestidigitation

Another popular form of stage entertainment has always been magic—although there's no such thing as "real" magic, the ability to defy the laws of physics using supernatural means. There are tricks that *appear* to be magic, however, and they come in two forms: legerdemain and prestidigitation. Although these terms are often used interchangeably nowadays, actual practitioners consider them to be two distinct arts.

Legerdemain is derived from the Latin *levis* for "light" and *manus* for "hand," and includes skills such as juggling and levitation, tricks that require some acrobatic skill and/or special props.

Prestidigitation comes from the Latin *praesto* for "prompt" and *digitus* for "finger," and embraces slight-of-hand entertainment such as card tricks and pulling quarters from kids' ears.

Basketball star Johnson obviously chose well when he selected the nickname "Magic," since both of the above obviously apply to his abilities!

Hoedown/Hootenanny

Not all live entertainment takes place in a theater, and high on the list of uniquely American amusements is the town-wide party, a tradition since the early nineteenth century. These celebrations usually take two forms.

A *hoedown* is a community party featuring organized square dancing. The word derives from the fact that one had to put the hoe down to dance—which involved men and women both, as hoes were used not only for tilling but for baking hoecakes. Hoedowns were held in New England, in the Midwest, and the South, though the latter was also partial to . . .

The *hootenanny*, a community get-together where the emphasis is on organized music making, usually on the fiddle, guitar, washboard, and piano, with dancing occurring spontaneously whenever the mood strikes. The word comes from the expression "hootin' Annie," Annie perhaps meaning the blackbird Ani, whose cries the revelers unintentionally mimicked.

Celebration/Jamboree/Party

Everybody knows what a *party* is. Whether it's a birthday party, a frat-house party, a going-away party, or a retirement party, it's a social gathering held to honor some special event, almost always providing refreshments, and often offering entertainment and games.

A *celebration* also commemorates a special day or event, but it's longer and bigger than a party and is usually broken down into scheduled periods of festivities—for example, a Fourth of July celebration, which sets aside a certain time for fireworks.

A *jamboree* is a gathering of people—typically, children—in which they pat themselves on the back for what they are, be it Boy Scouts, young athletes, or Mouseketeers. Organized festivities and a lot of food are a part of any jamboree.

These are all fun gatherings, with noise, food, and frolic. For those who are interested in a more sedate kind of get-together, however, there are . . .

Ball/Masque/Masquerade

It's likely that no one would even know the word "masque" these days if Edgar Allan Poe hadn't immortalized one in his 1842 short story, "The Masque of the Red Death." Yet that popular tale also helped foster the misconception that a masque and a ball are the same thing, since Poe's masque occurs at a ball.

A *ball* is a big, lavish party where there's a great deal of social dancing and food served on trays or in a buffet. The word "ball" is derived from the Old French word *baller*, "to dance."

A *masque* is an elaborate entertainment that, until early in this century, was performed primarily by amateur actors, usually in costume. Originating in England in the early seventeenth century, masques consisted of everything from skits to acrobatics to music, which were sometimes united by a theme. Masques were often performed at balls and other large public or private gatherings.

A masque differs from a *masquerade*, which is simply a ball in which all the partygoers dress up in costumes and/or masks. Both words are derived from the Spanish root *mascara*, or "mask."

Now for those interested in gatherings where costumes and often even clothing frequently were not necessarily a part . . .

Orgy/Saturnalia

The origins of both of these forms of public revelry are the same: to celebrate the success of the crop and the productivity of the land. However, the difference between them is in the expression.

An *orgy* is a party characterized by unrestrained sexual activity as well as drinking, dancing, and other indulgences. Orgies originated in ancient Greece, where they were held to worship Dionysus and Demeter—respectively, the god of fertility, wine, and drama, and the goddess of agriculture (and, ironically, the protector of marriage).

A *saturnalia* is a gathering where there is excessive drinking, eating, and dancing, although not necessarily sexual intercourse. It was originally held by the Romans to honor Saturn, the god of agriculture.

It's believed that the Greeks emphasized sex because the goddess of fertility was watching and she might see fit to make the Greeks fecund. And if not, they probably reasoned, what had they lost?

SPORTS AND
FITNESS

Amphitheater/Arena/Hippodrome/Stadium

Throughout most of recorded history, there has always been a place for professional athletes to compete against other athletes, whether the sport is football, baseball, basketball, boxing, or chariot racing. However, where they went depended on what they had to do there.

Originally, an *arena* was the oval area in the center of the outdoor theaters in Rome where games were held. Later, it came to mean any area or platform, surrounded by seats, in which a sporting event took place. The word is also sometimes used to describe the building that houses an arena, but when the word is used this way, the arena *always* has a roof.

More accurately, though, the building that houses an arena is called an *amphitheater*—unless it's oval or horseshoe shaped, in which case it's called a *stadium*. Both amphitheaters and stadiums can be built with or without a roof.

If horses run or perform in an amphitheater, then it's called a *hippodrome*; if the horses race over an artificial course, with ditches, fences, and other obstacles, the course itself is called a *steeplechase* (see *Spire/Steeple*, page 22).

Since Yankee Amphitheater and Belmont Hippodrome have a ponderous sound to them, many of these words are used interchangeably these days. Ironically, at the same time the showplaces are losing their identities, the events themselves are becoming more and more specific—for instance, American football as opposed to Canadian football, handicap races instead of stakes races, and . . .

Auto Race/Drag Race/Stock Car Race

In the language of race car drivers, an *auto race* is not just a race between automobiles. It's a race between sleek, customized, low-slung race cars that travel at high speeds, usually for several hundred laps over an oval track many miles long. A *grand prix* auto race is a race held at a number of international locales, outside of a stadium, and over long, difficult courses.

A *stock car race* is a competition between standard automobiles—Buicks, Chevys, and such—that have been converted for racing purposes. The course they run is usually a long oval.

A *drag race* is a short race between two or more cars of any kind—though typically not race cars—starting from a standstill. The course, or dragstrip, can be either straight or curved.

Lariat/Lasso

Another crowd pleaser in some areas of the country, rodeos are a showcase for the riding and roping talents of cowboys, and a place where it's literally acceptable to tie one on.

According to the old Walt Disney cartoon, more than anything a cowboy needs a rope, needs a rope, needs a rope. But strictly speaking, what he needs is anything with a noose . . . and that isn't necessarily a rope.

A *lariat* (*aka* a *riata*) is a long rope with a running noose at the end, one that tightens when pulled; it's used to catch horses or livestock. The term can also be used to describe any rope used for tethering animals.

A *lasso* is the same thing with one difference: although it can be made of rope, it can also be made of rawhide, leather, or some other material.

Of course, from the cow's point of view, all of this is academic. As far as it's concerned, no noose is good noose!

Skeet Shooting/Trapshooting

Like the rodeo, shooting is a controversial sport, especially when it involves the shooting of animals for sport. One way to sidestep all the wrangling is to shoot at nonliving things—for instance:

Trapshooting, an activity in which disks of baked clay (called clay pigeons) are flung into the air from a device called a trap and then shot down. Unless someone is hit by the subsequent flying shards, it's perfectly safe.

Skeet shooting is a form of trapshooting in which the targets or skeet (a dialectal form of "scatter") are launched at different elevations and speeds, to simulate the flight of game birds.

Another way to avoid shouting matches with animal rights activists is to take up one of these and attack another person instead of an animal. . . .

Épée/Foil/Rapier/Saber

As a weapon, the sword reigned until the seventeenth century; in Europe, duels were still fought by sword until the early years of the nineteenth century. Today, there are four kinds of swords, averaging thirty to thirty-four inches long and used solely for fencing.

In the sixteenth and seventeenth centuries, a *rapier* was a heavy sword with a double-edged blade used for thrusting and slashing. Because of its weight, however, the rapier tended to tire a wielder's arm rather quickly. Thus, in the eighteenth century, it was reduced in width and used solely for thrusting. The latter is the rapier now used in fencing.

A *saber* is one of two kinds of swords. When carried by soldiers, it was a heavy, single-edged sword with a slightly curved blade. In fencing, it's a double-edged sword somewhat heavier than a rapier (although lighter than the old military rapiers). The fencing saber has a distinctive hand guard that reaches from the bottom of the hilt to its top.

An *épée* is a rapier with a three-sided (triangular) blade; it's heavier and more rigid than the *foil*, a four-sided (square) rapier. Both have cuplike guards at the top of the hilt.

Billiards/Pool

Unless you fail to pay up on a bet, here's a safe, harmless sport.

Billiards is approximately six hundred years old, invented by the French when they brought lawn bowling inside (hence, the traditional green cloth that covers billiard tables).

Billiards is played with a cue stick, heavy at the bottom and tapering off to a fine end with a leather tip. In the U.S. and France, the game is played with three ivory balls, 2 3/8 inches in diameter, and with no pockets on the table; the object is to strike the balls and cushions in a particular order. In England, the table has six pockets and is similar to . . .

Pool, which evolved from billiards in the nineteenth century. Originally known as "pyramids" (from the shape of the racked balls), pool was played in England with players trying to knock the balls of opposing players into pockets—usually, each individual had three apiece. In the U.S., the objective was changed, as players tried to sink their own balls. The number of balls was increased to fifteen (seven colored, one black, seven striped), and a cueball was used to knock these into one of the table's six pockets.

There are various kinds of pool games, such as "sinking" the balls into pockets in succession, hitting any ball but naming the pocket it'll enter before the shot, playing only colored balls first and then striped balls, etc.

The term "pool" originated in the 1880s, when men, waiting for the results of horse races in parlors where pool betting was done, played billiards.

Perhaps the most important aspect of billiards or pool is knowing where the balls are going to go after they're hit. In other words, how they'll . . .

Carom/Ricochet

Remember the old TV cartoon character Ricochet Rabbit, the bunny sheriff who used to cry, "Ricochet and away!" before he went *ping ping ping*ing across the landscape to capture bad guys? If the creators had checked their dictionaries first, we might have had a totally different character ... or at least a different name.

A *ricochet* is a skip or rebound an object makes after hitting a glancing blow against a surface, which may or may not have been its target. A bullet striking concrete and bouncing off of it is a ricochet.

A *carom* is the rebound an object makes after it has first struck its *target*. In the game of pool, a carom shot would be hitting the cueball so that it strikes a cushion, bounces away, and hits a ball.

A ricochet is usually unexpected and its direction is unpredictable, whereas a carom is not. Since Ricochet Rabbit used his rebounds strategically, Carom Cottontail would have been a more accurate name.

Calisthenics/Isometrics

The Greeks believed that beauty (*kallas*) and strength (*sthenos*) went hand-in-hand, and the word *calisthenics* reflects that belief, coined to describe the kinds of gymnastic exercises that endow us with strength and grace, such as jumping jacks, situps, etc.

Isometrics, from the Greek *isometros*, "of equal measure," is a different kind of exercise, one in which there's no movement. The body is toned simply by tensing muscles one against the other or against a stationary object.

Although the Greeks, the fathers of the Olympics, pioneered these forms of fitness, more recent forms have evolved—a "-metric" conversion, you might say.

Aerobics/Anaerobics

Back in the fitness dark ages—in other words, before the jogging 1970s—the goal of exercise was largely to build muscle, or, in the case of recovering heart attack victims, to work out their cardiovascular systems.

Then the aerobics craze hit in the 1980s, and, contrary to the predictions of many pundits, it hasn't gone away.

Aerobics are any exercise that raise the pulse rate and intake of oxygen above normal levels, thus serving to condition the heart and lungs when continued for a lengthy time (at least twelve minutes). In general, aerobics burns fat.

Anaerobics is considerably more punishing, any form of exercise in which oxygen is burned off faster than the lungs can take it in, thus forcing the body to generate energy without it. This can only be accomplished for a short time before the oxygen debt rises so high that the face goes red, the limbs go slack, and the body finally collapses. You've heard of "crash and burn"? This is the opposite. In general, anaerobics builds muscle.

Theoretically, anaerobics increases the efficiency with which the body stores and burns oxygen. Unless you're planning to do some marathon running, however, stick to aerobics or some other form of exercise, such as . . .

Dumbbells/Barbells

Dumbbell takes its name from the apparatus that was used to ring church bells until the middle of this century—not the clapper (which, coincidentally, it does resemble), but the rigging that was raised and lowered to move the bell. This was a wooden (later, iron) pole with a weighted metal ball affixed to either end; pulling it enabled the bell ringer to sound the chimes without much exertion.

Late in the seventeenth century, someone noticed that these dumbbell pullers were getting kind of hunky, and the device was adapted for use as a muscle-building device. The first dumbbells were made to be used one in each hand; later, larger ones were made for two-handed lifting.

Because men with muscles quickly outgrew their dumbbells, the *barbell* was created, a bar to which replaceable disk-shaped weights could be attached.

Both dumbbells and barbells are known as *free weights*. If your role model is not Arnold Schwarzenegger but Steven Seagal, you might want to forgo the weights and take up one of these instead. . . .

Jiujitsu/Karate/Kung Fu/Tae Kwon Do

Jiujitsu was developed in the 1800s, when samurai (see entry, page 36) were no longer permitted to carry swords and had to find another way to protect themselves. They refined a form of combat that was over twenty centuries old: "the gentle art," which is based on immobilizing adversaries by placing them in arm locks or by dislocating or breaking their limbs. (Well, that *is* gentle, when compared to thrusting a sword through them.)

Karate literally means "empty hand," and was created on Okinawa shortly before the seventeenth century. In this form of martial arts, the side of the open hand is the primary weapon, and traditionally it was toughened by pounding it against tree trunks. Later, flying kicks were added to the repertoire in order to unhorse enemies. The practitioners, who were often farmers, also developed ways of using farm tools as weapons.

Kung fu was born in northern China around A.D. 520, in a Shaolin monastery. It means "person of the highest ability," and is a form of boxing with an emphasis on the palm of the hand as the chief weapon. Practitioners are taught not to attack first, but to respond to what an opponent does, the theory being that once a first strike has been neutralized, the attacker will be off balance and the defender can take advantage of any unprotected areas.

Tae kwon do means "the method of kicking with the feet and punching with the hand," and originated in Korea approximately 1,300 years ago. Though it evolved independently of the other martial arts, it uses the hand and feet in ways that are similar to karate.

Sauna/Steam Room/Turkish Bath

When you're finished with working out, it's time to unwind. Here are three different places where you can have a hot time in the ol' town:

A *steam room*, a room in which the temperature is kept constantly high by regular infusions of steam. The steam opens the pores, and the subsequent sweat washes away the dirt.

A *sauna* (*aka* a *Finnish bath*) was originally a steam room in which attendants treated visitors to gentle strokes from birch or cedar switches, which really opened the pores. Today, a sauna is a room in which heat is generated by hot rocks (often heated electrically) and steam is not present. (Nor are switch-bearing attendants!)

A *Turkish bath* is actually a three-step process in which the bather sits in a steam room, leaves and gets a rub-down, then steps into a near-freezing shower. The theory behind the Turkish bath is that the body is cleaned, then re-laxed, and then revitalized by cold water.

Turkish baths are said to have been introduced by the Romans to the Seljuks, who invaded the Byzantine arm of the Roman Empire in the eleventh century. The cold water appears to have been an "improvement" created just for the conquerors.

TRAVEL AND TRANSPORTATION

Argosy/Odyssey

Sometimes, ideas take hold that seem so sensible, no one questions them. For example, the widespread notion that the "odyssey" and "argosy" are even remotely similar.

They're not.

Thanks to Homer's account of the travels of the Greek hero Odysseus, an *odyssey* has come to describe any long, meandering journey, especially one filled with startling adventures, hardships, and danger.

It's widely assumed that "argosy" suggests an equally amazing and hazardous voyage, inspired by the travels of the Greek hero Jason aboard his ship the *Argo*. However, argosy and *Argo* have nothing in common other than four letters.

An *argosy* is a large merchant ship or fleet of ships, especially those with a rich cargo. The word comes from the Sicilian city of Ragusa, which was once a key mercantile center.

No doubt this is particularly distressing to those who thought the venerable old short story magazine was called *Argosy* because it was an adventure in literature. Turns out the publisher was just bragging!

Boat/Ship

Having settled the question of what an argosy is, here's another: What exactly was the *Argo*? Was it a boat or a ship?

Landlubbers tend to use the words indiscriminately, though someone who owns a ship may want to keelhaul anyone who calls it a boat.

Technically, a *boat* is any vessel that travels on water, is shaped to provide stability, and is equipped with some means of propulsion. However, among seafarers, a boat is any small vessel used for specialized purposes, such as a lifeboat, rowboat, or fishing boat.

A *ship*, on the other hand, is a large vessel usually used for long ocean voyages. Yet real men of the sea scoff at even *that* definition, insisting that a ship can only be a vessel with three or more masts, square-rigged and having jibs, staysails, and a spanker. Perhaps *that* explains why the ship of state is always so full of air.

And what happens if either a boat or a ship runs into trouble at sea? Then the result is usually one or both of these. . . .

Flotsam/Jetsam

Though the words are usually linked together, flotsam and jetsam are two very different things.

Jetsam, a colloquialized form of "jettison," is typically the first to hit the water: it's the cargo and contents of a ship that are thrown overboard in an effort to lighten or stabilize a vessel during an emergency. Regardless of whether the items sink or wash ashore, they're jetsam.

Flotsam, from the Old English *flotian*, "to float," is the part of a ship and its cargo that's left floating on the water or is washed ashore *after* the ship is wrecked or goes down. Jetsam can become flotsam, although not vice versa.

If you're not a participant in a tragedy at sea, chances are good you'll still see at least small pieces of flotsam and jetsam if you're standing on or by one of these. . . .

Dock/Pier/Wharf

Did Otis Redding err when he sang about sitting on the dock of the bay? He did . . . unless he had his bathing suit on.

A *dock* isn't any kind of structure at all: it's the water beside or between the piers and the wharves. Otis probably was sitting on one of *these* two structures: a *pier*, which is a rampway that extends from the land over the water, or a *wharf*, which is a walkway built along the shore.

Both of these structures can be built from wood, cement, or stone, although wharves built from masonry of any kind are usually called *quays*.

Now, staying on dry land for a while . . .

Cart/Wagon

The expression, "Don't put the cart before the horse" makes more sense than many people realize. Not only won't it go anywhere, but it'll fall down! Even though a wagon with the horse behind won't go anywhere, at least it'll remain upright!

Both are used for hauling and are drawn by animals, but a *cart* is any two-wheeled vehicle drawn by a horse, mule, or sometimes an ox. It can be heavy or light, often has springs, and is rarely covered.

A *wagon* is a heavier form of conveyance. It has four wheels (so it can stand on its own), is usually open (the exception being a *covered wagon*), and is usually pulled by a horse.

The two differ from *carriages* in that the latter are usually two-wheelers used to transport people exclusively, although certain kinds of carriages, such as *buckboards*, have four wheels and can also carry a small amount of cargo. A *coach* is a heavier four-wheeler, which is also used to carry people. Both carriages and coaches are almost always covered.

So why is the four-wheeled recreational vehicle called a go-*cart* instead of a go-*wagon*? You know how it is—someone's always putting the horsepower before the cart.

Blimp/Dirigible/Zeppelin

What made the *Hindenburg* a zeppelin while the Goodyear blimp is not? It's much more than the fact that the

Hindenburg was filled with highly flammable hydrogen, while the Goodyear blimp uses safe helium.

Both of them are "airships," but *zeppelins* and *dirigibles* are rigid airships. They've both got a metal framework covered with fabric; inside the framework are separate envelopes filled with the lighter-than-air gases that enable the airships to rise. The only major difference between dirigibles and zeppelins (which are named for aeronautical engineer Count Ferdinand von Zeppelin) is that the latter are some twenty-five percent longer. Able to hold hundreds of passengers, zeppelins were thus both quicker and more comfortable than ocean liners.

Blimps—a term derived from "Type B-limp," describing their condition when deflated—are nonrigid airships that were developed in the wake of the *Hindenburg* disaster (1937). There's no framework inside: let out the helium and all you have is a mass of canvas and rubber.

And no heavenly camera position for Sunday afternoon football games.

Inn/Hotel/Motel

During the Middle Ages, long before there was a Conrad Hilton or Leona Helmsley, *in* (*sic*) meant "house" in Old English, and an *inn* was any dwelling, public or private. Sometime during this era, people in the country who had large enough homes would pick up some extra money by opening a room or two for people passing through, and inn came to describe any establishment that provided shelter and food to travelers.

The *hotel* did not grow out of the inn, but from the concept of the hostel, a supervised lodging place for young people in a large town or city; both words (along with hospital) take their names from the Late Latin *hospitale*, or "guest room." A hotel is a large establishment, still found primarily in cities, that typically provides food and lodging, as well as shops and other amenities, for travelers.

The *motel* is a "motor hotel," a modern-day inn. Unlike hotels, motels usually provide parking next to the room, so lodgers can get up and go. Also, motels rarely have restaurants; about all you can buy there are snacks and knick-knacks sold from vending machines, or . . .

Postcard/Postal Card

If you buy a cardboard photograph of Disneyland, write a note on the back, buy a postage stamp, and mail it to a friend or relative, what you've sent is a *postcard* or *picture postcard*. It can measure any size, as long as it's commercially printed.

Only the United States Postal Service can issue a *postal card*, a 3-x-5⅛-inch card that has the postage printed on the front and the message sides completely blank. The first postal card was issued May 1, 1873, and although postal cards are white nowadays, this one was light buff with brown printing.

Suppose you buy a postcard and *don't* send it, but keep it for yourself. What is it then?

Memento/Souvenir

A *memento* is a keepsake of a person or event that has come and gone—for example, a locket once owned by a beloved aunt or the autograph of a celebrity you happened to meet.

A *souvenir* is an item kept as a reminder of a place visited—a place that's still there, even though you aren't. Souvenirs are usually manufactured expressly for that purpose, such as that postcard you bought for yourself of Disneyland or a replica of the Statue of Liberty . . . although it can also be a rock from the Grand Canyon, sand from the Sahara Desert, or a seashell from Hawaii.

Speaking of which, let's move on to some of the sights you might see if you were to travel around the world. . . .

THE GREAT OUTDOORS

Dusk/Sunset/Twilight

One of the pleasures of our little spot in the universe is the beauty of a setting sun. This daily spectacle consists of three separate phases, and apart from the fact that *The Dusk Zone* is a rotten name for a TV series, what's the difference between them?

Sunset is that period of the afternoon when the sun begins to disappear below the horizon, while *twilight* occurs when the sun is below the horizon and the light reaching our eyes is soft and diffused. Twilight can also be used to describe such conditions in the morning, and, by extension, anything in the sun's waning phase or any area between light and dark.

Dusk is the dark part of twilight in the evening, just as *dawn* is the bright part of twilight in the morning.

Forest/Grove/Woods

Composer Stephen Sondheim once remarked that he called his musical *Into the Woods* because it has a darker feel than *Into the Forest*.

Mr. Sondheim knows of what he speaks. A *forest* is a large tract of land covered with trees and underbrush; in England, a forest also may include a pasture.

The *woods*, however, are a large and thick forest, usually with deep and thick underbrush. Light doesn't penetrate the canopy of leaves and branches in the woods as easily as it does in a forest.

And *Into the Grove* would have been a total washout, a *grove* being a small wood, usually without undergrowth of any kind. The word is also used to describe a small orchard.

Moving from heavily treed regions to those that are sparsely wooded, we find . . .

Field/Meadow/Plain/Savanna

A *field* is any open ground, especially one that's clear of anything but low grasses, and particularly one that's suitable for use as pasture, tilling, or even for building a baseball diamond.

A *meadow* is a field with taller and more bountiful grasses, used for pasture or as a hay field.

A *plain* is any stretch of level, open land that, typically, has sparse vegetation. No section of a plain is more than five hundred feet higher than its lowest section—although this still allows for some pretty sizable hills.

A *savanna* is a plain that's thick with coarse grasses and scattered trees, usually found in tropical regions.

The vegetation you may or may not find in any of these includes . . .

Bush/Shrub

The difference between a flower and a plant is easy: a plant is any member of the vegetable group of living things, and a flower is its blossoming part. A bush and a shrub are much more similar.

A *shrub* is a woody plant with several rigid stems that rise from just above the ground. A *bush* is larger than a shrub, and has just one stem with many branches rising from it, at or near the ground. Botanists also define a bush as a cluster of shrubs so close together that they appear to be a single plant.

At home, shrubs are used to line paths or gardens, whereas bushes, especially when in a row—that is to say, a hedge—can be used to mark the boundaries of one's property and/or keep out prying eyes.

Mushroom/Toadstool

They may not be lovely to look at, but you can say one thing nice on behalf of mushrooms: They *do* grow fast. Many types of mushrooms can literally grow overnight.

A *mushroom* is a large, edible fungus (a nonflowering plant containing no chlorophyll) that grows quickly and has a pileus (cap) perched atop a stalk supported by radiating gills. The mushroom is only the outward or "fruiting" structure of a much bigger fungus that grows underground, in rotting trees, etc.

A *toadstool* differs from a mushroom in two ways: The pileus tends to be larger and more umbrellalike, and any part of the fungus is poison. Supposedly, the word "toadstool" originated in medieval times when toads tended to perch on or near them in dark, dank places. Why toadstools in particular? Because the larger caps provided the animals with more support, and the edible mushrooms were usually harvested and eaten before the toads got to them!

Although mushrooms may not be appetizing to look at, the taste more than makes up for that. Likewise another product of the great outdoors: chewing gum!

Elastic/Gum/Latex/Rubber

It sounds like a paradox, but although rubber can be elastic, it isn't elastic. And although gum is rubbery, it's tougher than rubber and won't fall apart when you chew it.

Rubber is made by drying the milky sap (*latex*) of rubber trees and plants. When the sap dries, the rubber is elastic, capable of returning to its original length and shape after being stretched or twisted. However, it is not ...

Elastic, a material or fabric that's springy because it's been run through with a rubber strip, *aka* an elastic band.

Harder than rubber is another viscid substance exuded by some plants: *gum*. However, gum is stickier and tends to coagulate more quickly upon contact with the air, and forms a malleable but not elastic mass when mixed with water. Many kinds of gum have a natural flavor—mint, for example—and people who live in the tropics have always chewed it to keep their mouths moist.

Today, all of these substances can be made synthetically, with more or less of the elasticity that occurs in nature—and, where gum is concerned, longer-lasting flavor!

Bayou/Bog/Marsh/Swamp

Why do people get bogged down with work or swamped with work, but never marshed with work?

There's nothing in the etymology of any of the words to suggest an answer, although it's probably due to the "muck" factor: while all are wetlands, marshes tend not to be as dark and gooey as the others.

A *swamp* is wet, spongy land where many types of trees and other vegetation manage to grow; it would be accurate to describe a swamp as a wet forest. (Trees such as the bald cypress and tupelos that grow in wetlands keep from toppling over in the soft soil thanks to their broad trunks or flangelike projections that support them.)

A *bog* is also wet, spongy ground, but it's sparsely populated with trees and its soil is covered with decayed vegetable matter, especially moss. Bogs usually develop from ponds or lakes that have extremely poor drainage.

A *marsh* is an open, airy place that usually has lush grasses and cattails growing in it, and is covered with water most of the year.

A *bayou* is any stagnant body of water in which vegetation is sparse.

Decay/Decompose/Putrefy/Rot

One of the hallmarks of swamps and bogs is that humans rarely go there, meaning any vegetation that dies just sits there. Does that mean it rots, decays, putrefies, or decomposes? Usually, it endures all of the above, albeit at different stages.

To *rot* (or *decay*) is to break down completely and relatively uniformly as a result of a degenerative process, such as a lack of sunlight or the action of parasites. Typically, rotting happens to something that is newly dead.

To *decompose* is to separate or settle into constituent

parts, usually slowly and as a result of pervasive rot. A rotting log still looks like a log; a log that has decomposed looks like a pile of soggy splinters.

To *putrefy* is to decompose through the action of bacteria and fungi.

It's curious that one of our most familiar curses, "Rot in hell!" isn't what we want at all. What we mean is for someone to stagnate in hell, which isn't the same thing. If something stagnates, it doesn't grow or decay; if they rot, their stay (and suffering) will be brief.

And while we're on the subject of rotting . . .

Compost/Mulch

Not all rot and decomposition is bad. To the contrary, in fact.

Thanks to society's increasing awareness of recycling, certain kinds of organic matter that came from the earth are now being widely returned to it, albeit in two different ways.

Compost is a mixture of decaying organic substances such as leaves and manure, which are used as fertilizer.

Mulch is straw, leaves, manure, or a combination thereof that is spread on the ground around vegetation *before* rotting, in order to prevent erosion, evaporation, and to enrich the soil.

Compost can be used as mulch, although the less decayed the vegetation is, the better it protects the soil by not washing or blowing away.

Fire/Flame

Another force that tears things down, though much quicker than decomposition, is incineration.

According to the fossil record—human and animal bones found near campfires—people have been using fire for at least 2.5 million years. We learned very early that three things are needed to make it: fuel, oxygen, and heat. As the fuel is heated (by rubbing it quickly, striking it with flint, etc.), its surface molecules begin to move very quickly, causing them to combine with the oxygen around them. This process and state of combustion is *fire*, the physical manifestation of which is . . .

Flame, a stream of burning vapor or gas that is divided into three zones, which you can see clearly around a burning candle wick: the thin "inner zone" of unburned gas where fuel and oxygen have not yet merged; the colorful "middle zone" of partially consumed gas; and the invisible "outer zone" of diminishing heat. Hold your hand above a flame if you want to feel the latter. And if you do, you'll be wanting to experience one of these next. . . .

THE WEATHER

Chilly/Cool

Something is said to be "cold" if its temperature is lower than that of the body's. Usually, the word is taken to mean a temperature that's *considerably* lower. For temperatures a little less uncomfortable, there are alternatives.

Cool describes a moderate loss of heat that produces a feeling somewhere between warm and cold. Weather that is cool is generally not unpleasant.

Chilly, on the other hand, is when the temperature is low enough to produce a superficial or fleeting sensation of cold—i.e., a chill—although it is not as consistently uncomfortable as being cold. A cold wind, blowing intermittently, undoubtedly will produce a chill.

Perhaps the words can be best explained in a social situation. If you get a cool reception from someone, you might still have a person's eyes on you and their attention. If the reception is chilly, you'll be lucky to get that!

Fog/Mist

In 1980, there was a movie called *The Fog*, about a band of pirate ghosts who lived inside a crawling fog. Why does that title register higher on the eerie scale than *The Mist*? Because fog connotes a lack of visibility and a resultant feeling of helplessness.

Fog is a mass of water droplets or ice crystals that hug the surface of the earth like a quilt. There are four kinds of fog: *steam fog*, caused when water from the sea or soil evaporates and hits cold air; *advection fog*, the result of warm, humid air passing over a cool surface and causing the moisture to condense; *upslope fog*, caused by warm, moist air moving up a slope and hitting cool air higher up; and *radiation fog*, when warm, moist air cools and the water condenses.

Meteorologically speaking, *mist* is a thin fog of any kind, a collection of smaller water globules that cling together tenuously and float just above the ground.

By definition, if you're in a mist, you can still see up to a kilometer in any direction—clearly not a place for ghosts of any kind to hide.

Cyclone/Hurricane/Monsoon/ Tornado/Twister/Typhoon

What was it that sent Dorothy from Kansas to Oz: a cyclone or a tornado? Author L. Frank Baum called it a cyclone, but did the gales confuse him?

A *tornado* is a column of air that stretches down, funnellike, from a cumulonimbus cloud (the tall "thundercloud") and spins at speeds often in excess of three hundred miles an hour. The life span of tornadoes ranges from mere minutes to an hour or so, and their swath of destruction usually covers no more than a few miles. Most common to the central U.S. and Australia, tornadoes form around severe low pressure systems, and it's not just their rapid winds that cause destruction, but the high pressure inside buildings relative to the suddenly low pressure outside that they create.

A *cyclone* is a somewhat larger storm, reaching up to three hundred miles across. Its circular winds spin more slowly around their low pressure center, and rarely reach even half the ferocity of a tornado. A cyclone of tropical origin is called a *hurricane*; cyclones in the western Pacific are referred to as *typhoons*. A *monsoon* is a wind- and rainstorm that occurs seasonally in India and southern Asia.

The term *twister* applies to either a tornado or a small, powerful cyclone.

Tidal Wave/Tsunami

A tornado at sea is called a waterspout, but they tend to be short-lived and rarely come in contact with shipping. At or along the sea, it's the waves you have to watch out for.

Despite what countless dictionaries and encyclopedias say (except for *The Oxford English Dictionary*, which gets it right), and despite consistent misuse in the media, a *tidal wave* is not a monstrous wave, but any high water caused by the changing tides. When they're tossed by winds or storms, tidal waves *can* be big . . . but not more than fifteen feet or so.

The wave to worry about is the *tsunami*, from the Japanese *tsu* ("harbor") *nami* ("wave"). Produced by seaquakes or undersea volcanic eruptions, *these* are the unusually large waves, up to a hundred feet high—and the kind that can rearrange a shoreline. Fortunately, due to the fact that over seventy percent of the earth's surface is water, most of them merely huff and puff at sea, never reaching land.

On land, however, there are other kinds of waters to worry about. . . .

Deluge/Flood

Noah built his ark after God told him that he would "bring a flood of waters upon the earth." This event from the biblical Genesis is familiarly known as the Flood or the Deluge. But if the words mean different things, how can they both apply to that event?

A *flood* is an overflowing of water—sometimes sudden, sometimes not—over land that is not ordinarily submerged. It can be caused by a swollen river, a broken water main, or . . .

A *deluge*, a great downpouring of water, typically from rainfall or a burst dam.

While the words can describe mutually exclusive occurrences (for example, a deluge over the ocean wouldn't produce a flood), in Noah's case they relate to different phases of the same calamity.

GEOLOGY AND GEOGRAPHY

Epoch/Era/Period

Geologically speaking, there are millennia of difference between the two following measures of time.

An *era* is a time period marked by broad historical events. For example, the Cenozoic Era began seventy million years ago, immediately after the death of the dinosaurs, and includes everything that has happened to this day.

An *epoch* is a time period marked by distinctive, but smaller, events. The Cenozoic Era is divided into seven epochs, the last two of which are the Pleistocene (one million–10,000 years ago), which was dominated by the Ice Age, and the Recent (10,000–present), which is marked by the emergence of human civilization.

Geologists also use the term *period*, a measure of time defined by the formation of rock strata rather than by what is happening to the life-forms on top of those strata. Periods run more or less concurrently with epochs, for not coincidentally, what happens to the earth itself very much affects those who are upon it!

Lava/Magma

Throughout its four-billion-year history, the earth has always been geologically active, for which we should be thankful: some scientists believe that life originated at the bottom of the oceans, where the building blocks of life were warmed and nurtured by vents in the seafloors.

A cause or result of the heat (scientists aren't sure which) are the seas of *magma* that fill the interior of our planet, molten material—primarily rock and metals such as nickel and iron—that solidifies when it is pushed upward, toward the temperatures considerably cooler than the estimated 7,000°F found at the center of the earth.

Magma comes from the Greek *magma*, or "a kneaded mass"; solidified magma is known as *igneous rock.*

When magma builds up in pockets under the earth's crust and erupts through a volcanic crater or vent *before* it can harden, the outpouring is called *lava.* The average temperature of lava is a balmy 2,000°F, and, depending upon its composition—thick or runny—it may harden quickly or flow for many miles.

Lava comes from the Latin *labi,* "to slide," about which the Italians of Pompeii unfortunately knew a great deal.

Gasoline/Grease/Oil/Petroleum/Tar

Not everything made inside the earth is bad for us, although it's ironic that so much of the world's economy is driven by rot—literally.

Petroleum (aka oil) is a thick, flammable, dark liquid. When it's a liquefied form of bitumen (asphalt or a similar substance), it's known as *mineral oil.* When it's formed by the decay and compacting, over millennia, of animal and vegetable remains, it's known as *crude oil.*

Petroleum doesn't mix with water and is used for lubricating and combustion; crude oil can be distilled into kerosene, benzene, paraffin, and other substances. Chief among these is *gasoline,* a flammable liquid used as fuel for internal-combustion engines. (*Petrol* is not raw petroleum, but simply the British word for gasoline.)

Grease was originally the melted fat of animals, although now it, too, is a byproduct of mineral or crude oil, and is used as a lubricant.

Tar is a dark, sticky substance that occurs naturally in nature, the result of the compression and distillation of coal and other organic materials, such as wood.

Pound for pound, the earth produces substances that are even more valuable, namely . . .

Gem/Precious Stone

The road to becoming a gem begins with rocks being subjected to unimaginable heat and pressure over eons, pressure that causes crystals to form. Depending on the components present during this melding process, minerals take on different colors: quartz with small traces of iron, for example, becomes amethyst, while corundum shot through with titanium becomes sapphire.

A *precious stone* is any such crystallike mineral—a ruby, diamond, emerald, sapphire, etc.—that is sufficiently rare and beautiful to be used in jewelry. Precious stones are typified by their transparency, dazzling colors, and hardness.

A *gem* is one of two things: a cut or polished precious stone or semiprecious stone (such as turquoise and garnet) ready for your neck, finger, or wrist; or a pearl (which is an animal product, not a mineral) that's fine enough to be used in jewelry.

Also highly valued, of course, are precious metals; unlike diamonds—which, according to the old Leo Robin/Jule Styne song, are a girl's best friend—men seem to prefer gold, silver, and platinum. Which makes sense: these can be spent or bent, qualities that satisfy that sex's characteristic impatience!

Boulder/Pebble/Rock/Stone

If you've got quartz in your timepiece instead of numbers, you've got a rock around the clock . . . or *do* you? To answer that, we first have to look at:

A *stone*, a clump of nonmetallic material made of minerals—hard, inorganic substances—that have been pressed together or simply accreted over the millennia.

A small stone, smoothed by years of erosion or by someone chipping away at it, is a *pebble*. So what you actually have in your clock are quartz pebbles.

A *rock* is a large group of stones—often of different compositions—that have been forced together by heat, pressure, erosion, or other natural forces, and that often have various metals mixed in. Peaks and cliffs are made of rock.

A *boulder* is a very large rock that is usually rounded

due to erosion and generally detached from a larger mass (such as a peak) and sitting all by itself.

And on the opposite end of the size scale we find . . .

Dirt/Sand/Soil

Here's the dirt on what happens to pebbles, stones, rocks, and boulders that have been around long enough to feel the bite of wind, water, and other erosive forces:

Soil is that part of the earth's surface comprised of disintegrated rock and humus (decomposed vegetable and animal matter).

Dirt is loose soil that is blown, kicked, or gets stuck where it isn't wanted.

Sand, like soil, is a disintegrated portion of the earth's surface, but in this case grains of rock, primarily quartz. (*Quicksand*, incidentally, is nothing but an ordinary pit of sand that's become saturated with water from an underground source. The water forces the grains apart, creating a muddy mix in which one can neither stand nor swim.)

But the forces that erode also build, and nature has ways of making these particles a piece of something larger once more. . . .

Agglomerate/Conglomerate

An *agglomerate* is a collection or mass of things that have been tossed or packed together, usually in a chaotic fashion—such as diverse kinds of rock and dirt fused together by volcanic activity.

Conversely, a *conglomerate* is a neater package consisting of disparate elements that have been more thoroughly mixed, formed, or rounded. An agglomerate exposed to eons of softening by water and air could well become a conglomerate.

In business, a conglomerate is a corporation that has acquired other companies that are in related fields (movies, records, publishing) to provide a business synergy, or has bought them in diverse areas (oil, real estate, TV stations) to provide a balance if one area falters. Technically, the latter should be called an agglomeration, but why rock the boat?

Archipelago/Atoll/Continent/Island/Isle

If you could see a time-lapse movie of the earth, shot from space, you'd see the planet's land masses in continuous motion: rising, falling, drifting, and colliding. The earth is alive, and the land masses it creates come in various shapes and sizes.

A *continent* is easy to define: it's one of the seven biggest land masses, the smallest of which, Australia, is still a whopping 2,966,136 square miles; at 840,000 square miles, poor Greenland doesn't quite make the grade and is considered an island—albeit, the largest one in the world. Which brings us to:

An *island*, which is any land mass entirely surrounded by water, but not large enough to be a continent. If there is another defining factor, it's that continents tend to drift over time, never disappearing, while islands have a habit of rising or falling into the sea.

An *isle* is a particularly small island, while an *archipelago* is an island group; the term includes both the islands and the large body of water in which they sit.

An *atoll* is a low-lying island, a more or less circular reef around a lagoon. It forms when a sea mountain (usually volcanic) erodes to a point below the surface of the water and a fringe of coral (the remains of various sea animals) grows atop the crater until it rises above the water, forming a lagoon within its boundaries.

Ocean/Sea

The difference between an ocean and a sea is comparable to the difference between a continent and an island: an ocean is much bigger than a sea. An ocean also allows land to rise above it here and there, while a sea is defined by the land that surrounds it.

The *ocean* is the vast body of salt water that covers three-quarters of the earth's surface, and, for convenience, is divided into five regions. It ends at, but is not defined by, places where the continental shelf or plateaus allow continents or islands to reach above its surface. The boundaries of oceans are strictly the work of cartographers, and not nature.

A *sea*, on the other hand, is a large body of water marked off by very distinct land boundaries. For example, in Southeast Asia, the mainland and the islands of Malaysia manage to define eleven seas in a relatively small area, with the South China Sea, Java Sea, and Sulu Sea being among them.

The term sea is also, however, used poetically, not geographically, to describe all vast areas of waters, including oceans, even large lakes, and . . .

Bay/Cove/Gulf

Like oceans and seas, the difference between a gulf and bay is largely one of size, although size creates their other distinguishing characteristics.

A *gulf* is a large section of a sea or ocean that is enclosed on three sides by land, thus forming a body of water that is still big enough to generate its own currents and weather systems.

A *bay* is smaller than a gulf; it's an arm of a sea or ocean that forms an indentation in the shoreline that is no more than several miles wide at its mouth. A small bay is called a *cove*.

Because both a bay and a cove are sheltered by land, they are typically more temperate than a gulf.

The Scottish term *loch*, which many lexicographers take to mean "lake," is, in fact, a landlocked bay that only *looks* like a lake. Lochs are fed underground by the sea, which is how many people believe Loch Ness's reported monsters come and go unseen.

Channel/Sound/Strait

Though the ocean and sea, a gulf and a bay, are clearly different from one another, there are some distinctions in terms of bodies of water that work in theory but not always in practice, forcing lexicographers to cross the street when they see cartographers coming the other way.

For example, by definition:

A *channel* is a small sea that passes between two land masses and connects two bodies of water.

A *sound* is a narrower but still very wide stretch of water that passes between the mainland and an island, or between two large bodies of water.

A *strait* is a still narrower stretch of water that connects two large bodies of water.

In fact, however, Long Island Sound is fifty miles across at its widest point and the Bering Strait is also fifty miles across at its widest point. The English Channel, which is seventy miles across at its widest point, and Long Island Sound are both stretches of water that pass between a large land mass and an island—meaning the English Channel should be a sound!

These places and many others were misnamed because there were no international standards when they were christened.

And, lest you think that confusion is a thing of the past, the faux pas of the age of exploration at sea have been duplicated in the exploration of the heavens, resulting in different names for the same heavenly bodies, such as asteroids and planetoids, and for explorers such as cosmonauts and astronauts. As much as things change . . .

Bank/Beach/Coast/Shore

When you go to the beach, have you gone to the shore or the coast? Quite possibly, both.

A *shore* is the area of land covered by the tides of the ocean or sea (*seashore*), or a gulf, lake, sound, etc. When the tide is out, that marks the farthest outward reach of the shore; when the tide is in, that's the innermost edge of the shore. The expanse where the land and sea meet, at any given moment, is called the *shoreline*. The part of a shore covered with sand and pebbles is a *beach*.

A *coast* is an area that includes the shore *and* any compositionally similar land lying on the perpetually dry side of the tides. In other words, if the shore is one hundred yards of sand, and the sand continues inward another hundred yards before it hits rock, brush, or whatever, those two hundred yards combined are the coast. The point where the coast and shore meet is called the *coastline*.

A *bank* is a continuation of a riverbed or streambed, made of the same materials with one difference: it's not under water. Banks are usually sloped, which is how they stay dry.

(And though it has nothing to do with any of the above, why do they call dockside laborers *longshoremen*? Do they work exclusively on long shores? Not at all. They work *along* shores, the *a* having been lost over the years.)

Abutting/Adjacent/Adjoining

While we're on the subject of shores, lakes, and the like:

You see an advertisement for a house on two acres adjacent to the beach.

Great! you think. That means on a hot summer day, you can fall out of bed and into the water.

You go to look at the house, but when you arrive you find that there's a highway between the house and the water. Did the advertiser lie?

Afraid not. *Adjacent* means that something is near something else, but not necessarily in contact with it.

If you want a home that actually touches the beach, you've got to find an advertisement that says the two are *adjoining*. Hopefully, the two will also be *abutting*, which means to touch *and* end at. (If not, some of your property may be underwater!)

Lagoon/Lake/Pond/Pool

Thanks to the movies, lagoons have either a pleasantly exotic connotation (*The Blue Lagoon*) or an unpleasantly exotic one (*The Creature from the Black Lagoon*).

No doubt that's because lakes, ponds, or pools can be found worldwide, whereas lagoons are tied to the oceans, seas, or large rivers.

136

A *lagoon* is any small body of water that's somehow connected with a larger body—for example, the lagoon defined by an atoll (see entry, page 133), which is adjacent to the ocean or sea.

A *lake* is any large body of salt or fresh water that's completely surrounded by land. It usually exists by itself, created millennia ago by melting glaciers. Enough land rises to cut it off from flowing into the ocean, etc.

A *pond* is a body of water smaller than a lake but still surrounded by land. Ponds are often artificially formed.

A *pool* is a pond that's unusually still, generally because of thick, surrounding vegetation or steep banks.

Glacier/Iceberg/Ice Floe/Pack Ice

Ever since its brush with an iceberg in 1912 caused the liner *Titanic* to sink, massive towers of ice have captured the public fancy. Before that, they were known only by seafarers, whalers, and others who plied the northern waters.

Like tornadoes, volcanoes, and other forces of nature, icebergs possess an awesome and surreal beauty. But while their height and jagged lines make them imposing, they're not the only masses of ice one might encounter on a journey toward the poles.

An *iceberg* is a mountain of ice drifting in the Arctic seas and sometimes beyond—particularly, those that float into the much used shipping lanes of the North Atlantic. Icebergs can be hundreds of feet tall, although seventy to ninety percent of that height is always under water.

An *ice floe* is any large, *flat* mass of floating ice—an island of ice—which, in most cases, has broken away from *pack ice*, the much larger, permanent mass of ice that covers the Arctic Ocean.

A *glacier* is a landlocked formation, a massive accumulation of snow that has compacted over the years, become ice, and started creeping outward on land. Rock, sand, and clay that accumulates on or around a glacier as it advances is called a *moraine*.

Crevasse/Crevice/Fissure

Earthquakes are caused by the movement of tectonic plates, the plates that float on magma (see entry, page 129), and, buried beneath soil, rock, and us, comprise the earth's crust. When the plates build up enough pressure against one another, they suddenly shift, and the result is a *fissure*, a narrow crack on the surface of the earth. If a fissure is wide and deep it's a *crevasse*, although crevasses can also be caused by erosion and other natural forces.

Both terms are applied to similar phenomena on other planets or moons, and crevasse is also used to describe deep rifts in glacial ice.

A *crevice*—which, like crevasse, comes from the French verb *crever*, "to crack"—is the opposite of a crevasse. It's a small fissure, although the term can be used to describe a narrow pit or cleft in the surface of any object.

Cave/Cavern

When Professor Hardwigg and his expedition took a *Journey to the Centre of the Earth* in Jules Verne's 1864 novel, they entered the crater of an extinct volcano to begin their journey. After that, they traveled along tunnels, galleries, labyrinths, slopes, shafts, alleys, and so on—but never any caves or caverns.

Good for Verne: inside the earth, the explorers would have encountered neither.

A *cave* is a large hollow in the earth, usually in the side of a hill or mountain. It can go on for miles, but however long it is it remains more or less horizontal *and* above ground.

A *cavern* is a large cave that begins on the surface but then slopes down and lies mostly underground, at times following a diagonal and/or vertical course. Some caverns, of course, do have underground entrances, such as a *tunnel shaft*, etc.

Both words come from the Latin *cavum*, or "hole."

Now, moving from the depths to the heights . . .

Bluff/Cliff/Precipice/Slope

Something the Hardwigg expedition *did* encounter inside the earth were steep walls of rock, all of which can be categorized as follows:

A *cliff*, the high, steep, usually narrow face of any rocky mass.

A *precipice*, a cliff with a face that is vertical, almost vertical, or overhanging (that is, the top sticks out more than the bottom).

A *bluff*, a low cliff, headland, hill, etc., with a wide, steep face.

And a *slope*, the side of any low-lying hill. You can only walk down a slope; the rest have to be climbed.

You can find all of the above on a mountain or peak—a peak being a mountain with a pointed summit *or* the pointed top of a mountain.

One of the disadvantages of any of the above is that all are notoriously unstable—as you can well imagine. Rock, dirt, or snow on a slanted or vertical surface does tend to tweak the law of gravity.

And if gravity gets annoyed, then you have . . .

Avalanche/Landslide

If, for example, just boulders or snow (but not both together) are tumbling your way, you're seeing an *avalanche*.

If, however, a whole mountainside is coming down at you—rocks, dirt, trees, other hikers or skiers, buildings, the works—then you're witnessing a *landslide*. A *mudslide*, *rockslide*, or any other kind of "-slide," implies that while the major component is one particular material, it's bringing other things down with it.

In political parlance, a landslide retains this character, as it brings all ages, sexes, ethnic groups, etc., into the victor's camp . . . all usually broken and bloodied, it should be noted.

One exception to the rule is water: falling water isn't known as a water slide. (That's an amusement park attraction.) Water pouring from a ledge is . . .

Cascade/Cataract/Waterfall

Honeymooners who go to Niagara Falls are seeing more than just a pair of waterfalls (the American and the Horseshoe falls), which, together, spill ninety million gallons of water a minute over their limestone lips. They're also seeing a pair of cataracts.

A *waterfall* is any steep flow of water dropping from a height, usually along a cliff, bluff, etc. (see entry, page 139).

A *cascade* is a small waterfall that's usually one of a series of waterfalls, i.e., cascades.

In the case of Niagara, each falls is a *cataract*, a large, rushing waterfall. A cataract doesn't have to fall from as great a height as the majestic Angel Falls in Venezuela (3,212 feet): Niagara is "only" 182 and 173 feet (American and Horseshoe, respectively). Width and volume are also important to a cataract.

(Just how did cataract also come to mean a disease of the eye? They both come from the Greek *kataraktēs*, to "rush down"—or, in the case of the eye, to "come down," as a shade drawn over the eye.)

ANIMALS

Mammoth/Mastodon

Modern-day elephants are all descended from the small-trunked, three-foot-tall mammal *Moeritherium*, which lived some fifty million years ago, in the Eocene Epoch. Many intermediary forms appeared between then and now, such as the *Dinotherium* and the *Trilophodon*, but none are more famous than the mastodons and mammoths, which have been preserved in cave paintings as well as in tar pits and ice, the latter two allowing us to study well-preserved carcasses of both genera.

Mastodons lived in the forests of eastern North America, and were big, shaggy creatures with long tusks that curved upward and in toward the trunk. They ate vegetation, stood an average of nine feet tall at the shoulder, and lived in the Oligocene and Pleistocene epochs, roughly from thirty million years ago to as recently as ten thousand years ago.

Mammoths also had large, inward-curving tusks, but they lived the world over, and, except for the woolly mammoths of Europe and Siberia, were hairless. These vegetarian brutes stood an average of eleven feet tall at the shoulder and thrived during the Pleistocene Epoch.

Both animals died out due to the changing climate, but animals that we humans nearly caused to become extinct are . . .

Bison/Buffalo

If you've got a home where the buffalo roam, then you've also got a home where the bison roam . . . as long as you're in North America. (Unfortunately, too many homes where the buffalo roam nearly doomed them to extinction, although conservation efforts in the early 1900s have helped to replenish their numbers.)

Buffalo are several types of large wild oxen that stand seven feet tall at the shoulder, and, in North America, include a family of animals known as *bison*, whose heads are slightly larger, shoulders more humped, and coats more reddish than their shaggy kin. There are two kinds of bison, the Wood bison and the Plains bison (which has a slightly darker coat).

Overseas, among the long-horned African buffalo—the forest buffalo and cape buffalo—and the Old World water buffalo, the sole representative of the bison clan is the European wisent, *Bison bonasus*, which stands some five and a half feet tall at the shoulder and was thought to have been hunted to extinction in 1919, although survivors were later found in the USSR.

What's confusing is that Europeans don't consider American buffalo to be true buffalo at all but bison, since they don't look like the buffalo of Europe. And if that's not confusing enough, consider the matter of . . .

Caribou/Elk/Moose/Reindeer

Apart from the fact that "Rudolph the Red-Nosed Elk" doesn't sound particularly appealing, it's primarily size and geography that distinguish elks from moose from reindeer.

They're all deer and large ruminants, a family that also includes cattle and camels. *Moose* are the largest of them all, often standing seven and a half feet high at the shoulder. They live in North America and are characterized by extremely long legs, a big head, a loose flap of skin (a "bell"), which hangs from the neck, and, on the males only, a huge set of antlers.

Found in Europe and Asia, *elks* are close kin to the moose, but shaggier around the neck and shoulders than around the rest of the body, and—again, males only— boasting a big rack of antlers.

Reindeer are up to a foot smaller, live in the northern and arctic regions of Europe, and are closely related to the *caribou* of North America. Both male and female reindeer (and caribou) have a large set of antlers—although red noses are a rarity.

Bull/Cow/Cattle/Steer/Oxen

Is a cattle drive also a steer and an ox drive? Most often, yes.

Cattle are any domesticated members of the genus *Bos*, which includes cows, which are female cattle, and *steers*, which are castrated males. Uncastrated males, of course, are *bulls*.

Steers and *oxen* are the same animal, although steer usually applies to an animal raised for beef, while an ox is primarily a draft animal.

Horse/Mount/Steed

King Richard was in a rather desperate way on Bosworth Field when he cried, "A horse! a horse! my kingdom for a horse!" Ordinarily, as a king, he might have been more particular.

A *horse* is a big, solid-hoofed, quadrupedal herbivore that's either wild or domesticated. Had Richard not been so distraught, he might have called for a *mount*, which is any horse intended for riding; or more likely a *steed*, which is a spirited horse used for riding . . . and fighting, which Richard intended to do.

So while a horse is a horse, of course (of course!), make sure you don't ask for Mr. Ed when what you really want is Rosinante! And while you're at it, Sancho Panza, don't get stuck with one of these . . .

Ass/Donkey/Mule/Onager

"You're as stubborn as a mule," or so the saying goes. If you adamantly hold your ground, does that also mean you're also stubborn as a donkey? Or are you just being an ass?

An *ass* is a long-eared mammal, *Equus asinus*, which is

used as a beast of burden and is kin to the horse. A *jackass* is the male of the breed (no wisecracks, please), while *donkey* originally described a small (diminutive suffix "-kee"), grayish brown breed ("-dun"). However, that distinction has been lost and jackass and donkey are now synonymous.

Onager is a term originally used to describe wild asses found in central Asia, but has since come to describe any undomesticated donkey.

A *mule* is the offspring of a mare and a jackass, while a *hinny* is the offspring of a stallion and a female donkey—though nowadays, mule is generally used for both kinds of hybrid (obviously; who ever heard of a hinny?).

Naturally, jackass and mule aren't the only animals that have lent their names pejoratively to human beings. For example, we also have . . .

Boar/Hog/Pig/Sow/Swine

These portly mammals have been domesticated for at least five thousand years, although many kinds, such as the warthog, still live in the wild and are fierce, intelligent predators.

Wild or domesticated, they're all *swine*, artiodactyl (having an even number of toes on each foot), hoofed mammals (the hoofs protect the tips of their toes) with a large head, small eyes, a prominent snout, and a flat nose. The male of the species is called a *boar* and the female a *sow*; wild swine often have shaggy coats and powerful tusks.

A *hog* is any swine that weighs over 120 pounds, while a *pig* is a swine that weighs under 120 pounds. Though these terms can apply to wild or domesticated swine, they're usually used for the latter, since who bothers to weigh wild ones?

The relatively hairless domesticated breeds have a reputation for being filthy because they wallow in mud. That's a misconception. They take mud baths to stay cool and keep the flies off, and, in fact, are otherwise quite clean. They also are known to eat like—well, pigs, but that doesn't mean they're slobs. Rather, it means they aren't picky and will consume anything from grass to grasshoppers to meat and bones.

Mouse/Rat/Rodent

Two more disparaging terms are mouse and rat, both of which mean dramatically different things; that's surprising, considering how closely related the real-life animals are.

It has been argued that the rodent has had a greater impact on human life than any other mammal—including humans! Not only do they live in every part of the earth and eat a great deal of stored foods, but rat-spread typhus and other diseases have taken more lives than all of our wars combined. On the other hand, because of our many biological similarities, rats and mice are the animals most often used to find cures for human diseases.

A *rodent* is a squat, compact mammal with short legs and a tail. It's extremely intelligent and can learn simple skills (usually having to do with obtaining food). All rodents have long whiskers that are touch-sensitive.

There are two kinds of rodents: sciuromorphs (squirrel-like), which include beavers, gophers, woodchucks, squirrels, and others; and myomorphs (mouselike), which include lemmings, chinchillas, porcupines, hamsters, and other species including mice and rats.

A *mouse* is one of several Old or New World species of rodent that range from Australian hopping mice to Brazilian arboreal mice to the common house mouse. They are very small rodents distinguished by high-backed bodies (they look almost humpbacked), large, rounded- or almond-shaped ears, and fur that can be white, gray, black, light brown, dark brown, or any combination thereof. They range up to six inches in length, from nose to tail tip, and will run when a larger animal or human approaches. The term *murine* is used to describe a mouse or mice. (Did anybody realize that when they named the eyedrops?)

A *rat* is also one of many Old or New World species, from the Galapagos rice rat to the Andean swamp rat. They're distinguished by their long, lean bodies, large and pointed ears, very long tails, big and narrow teeth, and generally solid-colored coat of black, brown, or gray fur. Rats grow up to a foot long, from tip to tip, and are fiercer and more aggressive than mice: they don't run unless something is thrown at them, a larger predator attacks, or if the ship is sinking.

Mice and rats are both excellent climbers and are generally herbivorous, although they can be omnivorous if need be.

Contrary to popular misconception, bats are not rodents but belong to a different order, Chiroptera.

Hare/Jackrabbit/Rabbit

Like the prolific rodent families, there are many species of lagomorphs, largely herbivorous mammals with long ears, and eyes high on their heads and set sideways to give them a wide field of vision. Lagomorph hind legs are longer than their forelimbs, and the animals are entirely covered with fur—different shades of white, brown, gray, black, and sundry mixtures. The lagomorph nose has nostril slits that can be opened and closed with a flap of skin above them, thus giving the animal the appearance of winking when it sniffs. Lagomorphs live the world over, in all kinds of climates.

There are two kinds of lagomorphs: pikas, which are little rodentlike creatures, and Leporidae, the familiar rabbits and hares.

Hares are distinguished by their remarkable speed and agility. They're extremely lean and long, reaching up to twenty to thirty inches, and have ears that average eight inches long. Their young (leverets) are born highly developed, covered with fur, and with their eyes open. Conversely, puberty comes relatively late for the hare, occurring at one to two years.

The *jackrabbit* is any of the numerous large hares of western North America, typified by unusually long ears and even longer hind legs than Eastern hares. The ears are so long, in fact, that early settlers thought they were as much like jackasses as rabbits, hence the name.

Rabbits are different from hares in that they are shorter, averaging just a foot in length. They live in burrows rather than in the open, and, unlike hares, prefer to hide rather than try to outrun a foe (hence the expression, "Scared as a rabbit"). Their young (kittens) are born relatively immature, being both naked and blind, and are kept in strong grass nests known as warrens. Puberty, however, occurs within three to five months.

Farmers the world over consider rabbits to be dangerous pests because they eat so much and reproduce so prodigiously (up to ten million are captured each *year* in Argentina), which leads to another popular expression that compares sexually aggressive humans to rabbits. However, to the rest of the world, these soft, cute creatures will always be *bunny rabbits*, a term that derives from the Gaelic *bun* for bottom, alluding to the cottontails among the many species of rabbit.

Cur/Mongrel

The animal infestation of our language reached its peak not with donkeys, swine, rodents, or rabbits, but with dogs. Consider: dog-tired, to die like a dog, dog-eat-dog, hot dog, dog-eared, in the doghouse, dogfight, dog days, dogface, and, of course, calling one's enemy a dog, dirty dog, or cur. Not a mongrel, mind you; that's not insulting enough.

A *mongrel* is any animal or plant that results from cross-breeding; a mule (see entry, page 143), for example, is a mongrel. The word apparently derives from the Old English *gemang*, "a mixture."

For a more pointed dig, however, the vocabulary provides us with *cur*, which is not only a mongrel dog, but a dirty and unfriendly one at that. The word comes from the Middle English word *curren*, "to growl," which is what curs tend to do.

Bobcat/Lynx/Puma/Wildcat

There are just seven species of big cats—the lion, tiger, leopard, jaguar, snow leopard, clouded leopard, and cheetah—as opposed to twenty-eight different species of small cats.

Surprised? Cat got your tongue?

The species that are frequently confused with one another are:

The *bobcat*, which lives from southern Canada to southern Mexico and is active at twilight. It preys on small rodents and large ground birds. The bobcat's coat is barred and spotted, black on reddish brown, with a white underside and a black tail tip.

The *lynx*, which can be found around the world in forests and thick scrublands. Also a twilight hunter, it lives on rodents and smaller hoofed mammals and has a light brown coat with dark spots, a black-tipped tail, long black ear tufts, and two tassels on the throat.

The *puma (aka cougar* or *mountain lion)*, which inhabits eastern North America and southern Canada and can be found in forests, grasslands, or deserts. It, too, hunts at twilight, but pursues mammals of all sizes, from field mice to fully grown bucks. The puma's coat is gray-brown or black, and the animal itself is extremely slender.

The *wildcat*, which includes all breeds of domestic cats, and, thus, can be found the world over. However, the larger, undomesticated wildcats, which live in forests and in open savannas from western Europe to India and Africa, feed on small mammals and birds, and hunt only at night. The wildcat's coat is brown with black stripes.

Buzzard/Condor/Vulture

You're watching a western movie, and after the hero has plugged a puma that killed his horse, he makes his way through the prairie on foot. Buzzards circle overhead, hoping to eventually feed on his remains.

You're watching a jungle picture, and a hunter has been mauled by a lion. Vultures alight on a nearby branch, hoping to feed on his remains.

The birds look and act alike; in some cases, they are.

Vultures are indigenous to the Old World, members of the Accipitridae family (see next entry). Unlike their kinfolk, vultures are big, bald-headed birds that feed primarily on carrion.

A *buzzard* is also an accipitrine, a soaring Old World bird similar to the vulture except for weaker talons and a shorter but still strong bill. It, too, feeds on carrion. The confusion arises in the New World, where vultures are members of a different family, Cathartidae, but are popularly referred to as buzzards—even though they aren't. If that western movie was shot in the U.S., chances are the buzzards were actually vultures.

To complicate matters further, *condors* are also New World vultures. They are the largest flying birds in the Western Hemisphere, with wingspreads of up to ten feet. They, too, are frequently referred to as buzzards.

Eagle/Falcon/Hawk

When is a hawk not a hawk? When it's a falcon.

In one of those quirks of science, when animals were named before they were fully understood, birds like the sparrow hawk and pigeon hawk are actually falcons, not hawks. They're closely related—birds of a feather, you might say—but they're still not the same.

A *falcon* is any of numerous diurnal (daytime) birds of prey of the family Falconidae. Falcons have long, pointed wings that bend in the center to point backward, and a bill that is notched on its sides. They range from four inches (*falconets*) to seventeen inches long.

A *hawk* is also a diurnal bird of prey, this one of the family Accipitridae. It possesses a wider body, and wings that are generally at right angles from the body. Hawks range in length from twelve inches to nearly two feet; the larger accipitrine birds are called *eagles*, which reach up to a yard in length.

Most hawks and eagles soar as they hunt; falcons tend to sit on a perch and watch for prey. Due to their greater size, the big birds conserve energy by gliding on rising air currents rather than flapping their wings. (Perhaps they should take a cue from their cousin the vulture and wait for stray cowboys and hunters!)

As for flying creatures a little less majestic . . .

Bug/Insect

All bugs are insects, but not all insects are bugs. (All insects, however, are gross, and then some.)

Insects are invertebrates. What makes them different from spiders, scorpions, ticks, centipedes, and millipedes, however, is the fact that insects have bodies that are divided into three parts—a head, thorax, and abdomen—and they sport a pair of antennae. Almost all of them have three pairs of legs, and most have wings.

No one knows for certain where the word *bug* came from, though it appears to have been derived from the Middle English word *bugge*, a scarecrow. (The word "bogeyman" appears to have come from this root, too.) That makes sense, for bug was originally applied only to the *most* repulsive kinds of insects: beetles—which comprise forty percent of all insects—with cockroaches, grubs, and larvae thrown in for good measure.

Bug still means those things, although it's also now used with various defining words to denote specific kinds of insects, such as bedbugs and stinkbugs—thus upholding the word's repugnant tradition. (Those cute, brightly colored ladybugs are the exception.)

Bee/Hornet/Wasp/Yellow Jacket

As superhero names go, why does the Green Hornet have so much more sting than, say, the Yellow Bee? Why doesn't having a bee in one's bonnet sound *quite* as scary as having a wasp in one's bonnet?

That's because *bees* are fuzzy, black-and-yellow, thick-bodied workers who have comforting names like bumblebee and honeybee, and perform useful tasks such as pollinating flowers and producing honey (by mixing nectar with glandular secretions). They are hymenopterous insects, which means they've got membranous wings, and while some are loners—such as the leafcutting bee and carpenter bee—most live in highly organized colonies with a queen, workers (sterile females), and drones (males).

Contrary to popular belief, most bees tend to flee rather than sting when threatened, and most will attack only in defense of the hive. The reason? After leaving their barbed stinger in an enemy, a bee is literally ripped in two and dies. Moreover, only female bees can sting.

Wasps also belong to the order Hymenoptera. They are

also mostly social creatures, but are longer and more slender than bees, with narrow waists and a metallic-looking, hairless exterior. Unfortunately, the females can sting over and over and over again.

Hornets (aka yellow jackets) are exclusively social wasps that have a pecking order similar to bees. These black-and-yellow creatures are the runts of the family, and while smaller than most wasps, are far more aggressive: the ladies can and will sting repeatedly—at the slightest provocation.

Grasshopper/Locust

As much as bees frighten people on a one-to-one basis, and bunches of them also aren't much fun, no insect is more terrifying or destructive in a swarm than a member of the grasshopper family.

A *grasshopper* is any herbivorous insect of the order Orthoptera, which includes crickets and cockroaches and is characterized by leathery forewings and membranous hind wings. The grasshopper has two sturdy antennae, is distinguished by long hind legs adapted for leaping, and reaches an average length of two inches. A grasshopper will usually live alone unless it's a . . .

Locust, a smaller member of the grasshopper family, one that has shorter antennae and migrates in swarms. These swarms often number in the billions, and where they alight no vegetation survives. Inexplicably and tragically, migrating locusts respond to the "crowding" of swarms by bearing more young.

While we're on the subject of unpleasant creatures . . .

Reptile/Lizard

Either you love 'em or you hate 'em.

Scaly, beady-eyed *reptiles* are any cold-blooded vertebrates of the class Reptilia, which comprises turtles, snakes, crocodiles, the tuatara (a creature that's the last surviving member in its order, the Rhynchocephalians), and one more suborder: the Lacertilia, or *lizards*.

This last grouping, which includes the Gila monster,

iguana, and many others, is distinguished by its moderately long body (from six inches to six feet), a tapered tail, and two pairs of legs.

Virtually all languages have different words for reptiles and lizards, although the French have brought them together: both *lézard* and *reptile* are masculine nouns.

Terrapin/Tortoise/Turtle

These three breeds of reptile (see entry, page 151) are so similar that the popular characters could have been called Teenage Mutant Ninja Tortoises with hardly any change in their design.

Although *turtle* can also be used to describe the entire group of shelled creatures, terrapins and tortoises have several unique characteristics: the *terrapin* is a freshwater species that lives mostly in North America, while the *tortoise* is a land species with thick, elephantlike legs.

Exclusive of these, the *turtle* is any of the more than two hundred other species that may have flippers or claws, long snouts or round heads, small bodies or extremely large ones (weighing from a few ounces to five hundred pounds), be water or desert dwellers, etc.

Though certain breeds may nip at people, they aren't generally aggressive, which puts them several notches ahead of some fellow reptiles. . . .

Alligator/Crocodile

It was a crocodile that ate Captain Hook's hand in *Peter Pan*. Would an alligator have been so nasty?

Most definitely.

Both reptiles have thick, armorlike skin and look and act very much the same. But there are significant differences.

Crocodiles (from the Greek *krokodilos*, or "lizard") are much bigger, reaching up to twenty feet in length, and live in the sluggish waters of tropics worldwide.

Alligators (from the Spanish *el lagarto*, also "the lizard") live only in China and in the southeastern United States and reach a measly (!) eleven feet in length.

If size enough doesn't tip you off, you can tell who's who by their heads, which are shaped somewhat differently. An alligator's snout is broader and rounder, while more of a crocodile's teeth protrude when its mouth is shut, making the animal look fiercer.

But don't let appearance mislead you: *both* are killers that wouldn't hesitate to bite the hand that feeds them.

Still, their reputation is sterling compared to another group of reptiles, whose names are not only used to describe the lowest of humans, but who, according to the Bible, made a misery of life on earth.

Serpent/Snake/Viper

Here's a question you can use to win bets: How long is a snake's tail? Contrary to popular belief, a snake isn't all tail with just a head in front. Most snakes are all backbone and organs, with a head on one end and a very short tail (roughly ten percent of its body length) on the other.

Here's another question for winning bets: What's the difference between a snake, a serpent, and a viper? Answer: All are snakes, but there are some major differences.

A *snake* is any long, limbless, scaly reptile without movable eyelids (a clear cover protects the eye). Most have just one lung (it fits easier than two), and—believe it or not—very few snakes are venomous.

A *serpent* is a large snake, usually ranging from eight to thirty feet long (although there have been reports of aquatic anacondas in South America reaching up to fifty feet in length). Most of these, too, are nonvenomous.

A *viper* is one of many kinds of snake found in Europe, Asia, or Africa; it's also one of the pit vipers of the Americas, which are vipers with heat-detecting pits in their heads, such as copperheads and rattlesnakes. Vipers are easily recognized by their eyes, which have long, vertical, catlike pupils, and most bear their young live instead of laying eggs. Unfortunately, if you're close enough to check out their eyes or nest, chances are you'll discover one more thing about them: unlike their wriggly kin, *all* vipers are venomous.

Most crossword puzzle fans are familiar with the word "eft," the clue for which is usually, "A newt." However, all newts are not necessarily efts ... although they are all salamanders.

A *salamander* is a tailed amphibian with soft, moist, scaleless skin. It has an aquatic larval state, after which it undergoes immature and mature terrestrial stages. The full-grown salamander averages eight inches (although the Japanese giant salamander reaches five feet!) and often returns to the water during dry spells.

A *newt* is any of the small, brightly colored salamanders that live in North America, Europe, and parts of Asia.

Despite what countless dictionaries and even the *New York Times* crossword puzzle says, only a salamander or newt in its *immature* terrestrial phase is an *eft*, a word that came from "ewt," an old form of "newt."

In the Middle Ages, salamanders were frequently found in blacksmith shops, having graduated from their aquatic phase and gone to where it was dark. For this reason, and because they could regenerate lost body parts, salamanders were much feared as supernatural beings that lived in fire. (Not bad for a creature generally one-thirtieth the size of a crocodile!)

Frog/Toad

Back when we were talking about toadstools (see entry, page 122), we explained how they got their name. What we didn't tell you is the reason the fungus was called a toadstool instead of a frogstool in the first place. The answer is simple: Frogs don't even live where the toadstools are.

A *frog* is any of a number of tailless, smooth-skinned amphibians with long back legs that enable them to make big jumps. Most frogs live by ponds, creeks, swamps, and other perpetually wet areas.

A *toad* is a tailless amphibian related to the frog, although it has warty skin and lives on land (except for when it's very young and when it breeds). Toads can be found in woods, in sheds, or anywhere else that is dark . . . just like the fungus that bear its name.

Toads are slightly larger than frogs, and their skin is brownish as opposed to the green of frogs. However, both are tadpoles in their young, immature form, and croak primarily to attract a mate; this sound is amplified by the big, inflatable air sacs at their throats.

As the name implies, a *bullfrog* is a large, deep-voiced frog.

Dolphin/Porpoise

Although porpoises and dolphins are both cetaceans—marine mammals with big, complex brains, emotions, and, for most, the ability to communicate—they're physically distinct from each other.

There are six types of cetaceans classified as *porpoises*, mammals with a torpedo-shaped body, spade-shaped teeth, and a blunt, rounded snout. Porpoises average four to five feet in length, and are generally smaller than dolphins.

Dolphins possess a larger, fish-shaped body, peglike teeth, and a head that ends in a beaklike snout. There are thirty-seven species of dolphin, which range from five to thirty feet long.

The problem is, when scientists aren't using the many genus and family names, they tend not to be too fussy about the distinctions between porpoises and dolphins. In most European countries, they're generally referred to as dolphins, while it's just the opposite both here and in Great Britain.

Increasingly, though, the dolphin advocates are winning out, despite the fact that there are two kinds of fish also called the dolphin. One wonders what the animals themselves would choose if anyone bothered to ask. . . .

Shrimp/Prawn

Shrimps and prawns are both slender, long-tailed decapods (ten legs) with four antennae—two of which are extremely long—and a shieldlike shell.

Because shrimps happen to live where a lot of fishing is done, more shrimps than prawns end up on barbecue skewers. But that isn't the only difference between these two little sea creatures.

Shrimp derives from the Middle High German *schrimpfen*, which means "to contract." The crustacean lives exclusively in salt water (which is why so many are caught) and averages two inches in length.

Prawn comes from the late Middle English *prane*, a word with no known meaning other than to describe the crustacean. The prawn has a distinctive upward-pointing snout, lives in either fresh or salt water, and averages three to four inches in length.

That's the long, the short, and the shorter of it!

Ermine/Mink/Sable

One thing these mammals have in common is that, incredibly and sadly, people still make coats from their pelts. Other than that, they're rather different creatures.

An *ermine* is an Old World weasel that lives in the forests of North America and Europe and in some of the warmer climes of Africa and Asia. It has a brown-and-white coat, except for in the winter, when its coat is white. Its tail is black-tipped year-round.

A *mink* is a weasellike, semiaquatic animal of North America and some parts of eastern Europe. The mink has a long, serpentine body, with a brown, lustrous coat.

A *sable* is a marten, another weasellike mammal, one that dwells in the colder regions of Asia and Japan and has a rich, darker brown coat. (It is unknown why the color "sable" is black, not brown.)

If we can't tell you why these cute little creatures are butchered for their skins (artificial furs are warm and dressy), we can tell you whether they've been killed for their pelts or hides. . . .

Hide/Pelt

Reportedly, John Lennon once declined to wear fox trim on a jacket because he felt it was immoral, and, besides, didn't want to rock the audience with pelts.

The tale may be apocryphal, but these tails—and backs and sides—are very real.

A *pelt* is the skin of a small animal, such as a fox, rabbit, or mink.

A *hide* is the pelt of a larger animal, such as a buffalo, deer, lion, cow, etc.

The terms apply whether the skin is raw or dressed.

What would be interesting would be to let everyone who wants to wear an animal hide do so—provided they harvest it themselves and it's a lion skin. Folks would quickly become content with cloth jackets, and at the same time learn the difference between . . .

Domesticate/Tame

Cecil B. DeMille said it best when he was making his circus picture, *The Greatest Show on Earth*: "You can tame a lion, but you can never domesticate it."

To *domesticate* is to accustom an animal to life in or around people, at a home or a farm. A domesticated animal may still have a hunter's instincts, and probably could survive in the wild, although it has no desire to return to the wild permanently. A dog or swine are examples of domesticated animals.

To *tame* is to train a wild animal to live among humans, although if the animal were allowed to return to the wild it would quickly shuck the veneer of domestication. A horse or a falcon are animals that can be tamed.

There's no word that expressly describes animals neither domesticated nor tamed but still living in captivity, but there are words to describe where you'll find them. . . .

Menagerie/Zoo

When Tennessee Williams wrote *The Glass Menagerie* in 1944, he chose the title for a reason: the most important figure in the delicate collection is a unicorn, a creature one could only find in a menagerie.

A *zoo*—a shortened form of *zoological garden*—is a park or similar grounds where live animals from all parts of the world are kept for public exhibition. Ideally, each animal's natural habitat is re-created as faithfully as possible, both for the welfare of the animal and the enlightenment of the public.

A *menagerie* is typically smaller than a zoo; it's either a private or a public compound for the exhibition of wild, dangerous, or exotic animals (which a unicorn certainly would be). Usually, however, the animals are not all of one kind, and specific names, such as an aquarium, apiary, and aviary are applied to such collections.

FOOD AND DRINK

Agriculture/Agronomy

Old MacDonald had a farm, and when he wasn't e-i-e-i-o'ing, he was busy planting a cover crop. Does that mean Farmer MacDonald was practicing agriculture or agronomy?

Agriculture is the science or skill of cultivating land and raising crops. The key word is "cultivating," which means tilling the soil, planting the seeds, then nurturing and reaping the crops. It can also include the raising of livestock and poultry.

Agronomy is the art or science of soil management, and involves maintaining the soil so that it doesn't become exhausted or washed or blown away, especially during its "downtime" in winter. That means using chemicals to enrich it, or, particularly in these days of "all-natural" farming, planting cover crops such as grass and rye to nourish the soil and keep it from blowing or washing away. Agronomy also includes working out efficient means of irrigation and drainage.

That makes Old MacDonald an agronomist, and the mind reels with the lyric possibilities ("With a pH here, and a pH there . . .").

Cabbage/Lettuce

One thing Old MacDonald would never do is confuse these two vegetables. They may look similar, and even mean the same thing to crooks—"green" or money—but in the garden they're two completely different things.

Cabbage is any vegetable of the mustard family, Bras-

159

sica, although the term is usually applied to the varieties with a short stem and thick leaves that are formed in a compact, edible head.

Lettuce, on the other hand, is a leafy herb of the Lactuca family. Although the word means the entire plant, it is commonly used to describe just the crisp, green leaves.

Technically, lettuce is actually closer to *spinach*, an herbaceous plant of the goosefoot family whose leaves are usually eaten cooked.

Now that we've gotten to the root of that problem, here's a problem with a root . . .

Sweet Potato/Yam

As Popeye the Sailor says, "I yam what I yam." Just make sure that the next time you fix a Thanksgiving dinner, *your* yam is a yam and not a sweet potato.

A *yam* is a brownish starchy tuber (a subterranean outgrowth of the stem) of vines of the genus *Dioscorea*. What are sometimes mistakenly called yams are actually *sweet potatoes*, which are the actual orange-colored roots (not tubers) of the morning glory *Ipomoea batatas*.

If most of us were to take the taste test, we might not be able to tell the two apart. However, that isn't true of these next folks, for whom food is more than simple sustenance. . . .

Epicure/Gourmand/Gourmet

It will come as no surprise that two of these words have French roots: gourmand from the Old French *gormant*, or "glutton," and gourmet from the Old French *gromet*, a "valet" in the employ of a wine merchant. Only epicure has a different origin, although the Greek philosopher for whom it was named was full of joie de vivre and would surely have lived in France were he alive today!

A *gourmand* is someone who is fond of eating, and tends to do a lot of it, often indiscriminately. A gourmand might enjoy a rich ice-cream sundae, for instance, and wouldn't necessarily know (or care) whether the ingredients were made of butterfat or ice milk. That's the role of . . .

The *gourmet*, a connoisseur of foods and all their subtleties. A gourmet cares less about filling his or her stomach than savoring the delicacies of the table. Originally, the word applied only to wine tasters, but it took on its broader meaning sometime in the eighteenth century.

An *epicure*, named for the Greek philosopher Epicurus, is also a gourmet, but one who appreciates the trappings of fine living as well, including music and art. He believed that the atoms themselves are arranged to afford us the highest pleasure, and, conveniently, by indulging ourselves we're simply following the wishes of nature.

No wonder he had more followers than his contemporary Zeno and the Stoics!

Appetite/Craving/Hunger

Like gourmands, rock 'n' rollers are big on hunger. Duran Duran was "Hungry Like the Wolf," Bruce Springsteen had a "Hungry Heart," and Paul Revere and the Raiders were "Hungry (for the Good Times, Baby)."

Why all this hunger, and so few cravings or appetites?

"It's probably because appetite has too many syllables for a song," says rocker Kirk Hammett of Metallica, "and craving sounds a little too nasty."

Right or not, it's something to chew on.

Hunger is a compelling need to have food (or, by extension, anything else), but it's still something that's under control.

Appetite, in addition to being a longer word, also suggests moderation (something that's inappropriate for a rock song!): it's a desire, fondness, or inclination to eat—or, again, to have anything.

As for *craving*, that's to desire something eagerly, even irrationally, be it food, attention—or, as Mr. Hammett puts it, something "nasty."

Biscuit/Brioche/Bun/English Muffin/ Muffin/Roll/Scone

Even if you're not a gourmand or gourmet, eating is obviously important, one of the first things we do every day of our lives.

If your tastes run to something on which you can spread some butter or margarine in the morning, you've got a number of choices.

A *roll* is a thin slab of dough, folded or doubled on itself before baking, so that it comes out in a domelike shape, with an exterior considerably harder than the interior.

A *bun* is dough baked like a roll, in round or oblong shapes, and often sweetened and/or spiced before baking. The outside is generally coated with melted fat or butter, so the crust comes out softer than a roll.

A *brioche* is a very light, sweet bun.

In England, a *biscuit* is synonymous with a cookie. On these shores, however, it's dough shaped into small cakes and raised with baking powder or soda instead of yeast, which gives them a different taste and texture.

One of the most popular morning foods is the *English muffin*. Although the ingredients are similar to the baked goods above, it's a more traditional breakfast food for one simple reason: In the days before toasters, they were flattened yeast dough cooked on a griddle, easily made alongside eggs, pancakes, bacon, etc.

The non-English *muffin* is a cake made, typically, from wheat flour or cornmeal, the dough having been mixed with blueberries, chocolate chips, bran, or the like.

Also from England is the *scone*, a flat, round, American-style biscuit made with oatmeal, wheat flour, barley, or a similar ingredient.

And if you're still hungry after all that (as a true gourmand would be), break out the griddle. Or is that a skillet?

Griddle/Pan/Saucepan/Skillet

You're not Julia Child, but you know the difference between bacon and eggs, and you know how to cook them.

The question is: Do you know what you're cooking them *in*?

If you're using a broad, shallow metal container—which, more often than not these days, is coated with a nonstick surface of some kind—it's a *pan*.

If the pan has very little depth it's a *griddle*, and if it has greater depth and (usually) comes with a cover, then it's a *saucepan*. If you're using a long-handled saucepan, then it's a *skillet*.

So you make your eggs and fat-free bacon, and before you know it it's time for lunch. You decide to avoid the kitchen and have a barbecue, and now the question becomes: What exactly are you cooking?

Frankfurter/Hot Dog/Wiener

In 1852, a group of butchers in Frankfurt, Germany, created a highly seasoned beef-and-pork sausage that came to be called the *frankfurter*.

Why did they bother? Because they were tired of stuffing little, membranous skins (and themselves) with the smaller, smoked *wienerwurst* ("Vienna sausage"), which lost the "wurst" part when it came to these shores. Today, especially little wieners are known as "cocktail franks."

As for *hot dog*, that's what you get when you put a frankfurter or wiener on a split bun: it's not the meat, but the whole sandwich. The etymology of hot dog is uncertain, though it arose at the turn of the century, either because of its resemblance to a dachshund or the rumor that many of them were being made from dog meat.

In case you were wondering, the average American eats forty hot dogs a year.

Bisque/Bouillabaisse/Broth/Chowder/
Fricassee/Soup/Stew

If it's a chilly day, you'll probably skip the barbecue and opt for something warm, such as . . .

Soup, a food made by placing fish, meat, vegetables, and

spices—alone or in combination—in a liquid such as water or milk, after which the mixture is boiled or simmered.

Broth, a thin soup made with meat or fish boiled in water, or of concentrated meat or fish stock diluted with water. Vegetables can also be part of the mix.

Bisque, a heavy cream soup usually made from pureed shellfish, game, or vegetables.

Bouillabaisse, a soup or stew also made with fish or shellfish, but thinner than bisque.

Chowder, also a thick soup and usually made with clam and vegetables, although it can be made with any fish.

Soup is usually served as an appetizer; a liquid entree gives you a bit more to chew on, to wit:

Stew, any preparation of meat and vegetables cooked by simmering in liquid of some kind—i.e., stewing.

The liquid content of stew is much less than in soup and is even less in a *fricassee*, which is chicken, veal, or another meat browned, stewed, and served in a white sauce made from its own stock.

But don't eat too much: dessert is still ahead.

Custard/Ice Cream/Ice Milk

When it's time for dessert, and you don't feel like frozen yogurt, there are some trusty old standards you can turn to.

Ice cream is still the favorite, a frozen dessert made of cream, then sweetened and flavored, with all the ingredients churned together slowly as they chill, causing it to thicken.

Ice milk is ice cream made with skimmed milk instead of cream.

Custard (*aka frozen custard*, or, incorrectly, *soft ice cream*) remains a favorite among children, a smooth, messy dessert made with less butterfat—often with skimmed milk—and churned less, so it has a softer consistency.

While we're on the subject, the difference between a *malted milk* and a *milk shake* is simply the addition of malt—a grain, usually barley, that has been steeped in water and dried in a kiln. Otherwise, the recipes are the same: whole milk, a flavoring, and ice cream whipped together in a blender.

Ices/Sherbet/Sorbet

If you want something a little lighter than ice cream or ice milk, there are some refreshing options.

Ices are made with sweetened water and fruit juice—although these days, many companies are using artificial flavors instead of real juice.

Sherbet (not sher*ber*t) is also made with sweetened water and fruit juice, although milk, egg whites, or gelatin are added to give it a creamier texture. In England, sherbet is a *drink* made with sweetened water and fruit juices.

Sorbet is just another way of saying sherbet, and it's usually referred to this way in fancy restaurants that serve small portions to cleanse the palate between courses.

Before leaving the sticky subject of fruit byproducts, let's have a look at . . .

Jam/Jelly/Marmalade/Preserves

Why do most people make peanut-butter-and-jelly sandwiches instead of peanut-butter-and-jam sandwiches?

Because *jelly* is a relatively thin, soft spread made by boiling fruit juice (or meat juice) with sugar and allowing it to cool. Because of the even, thin consistency of the juice, jelly tends not to stick together in globs, hence its popularity as a spread.

Jam is made the same way, but with slightly crushed fruit (fruit that's been "jammed down," as it were) instead of juice. As a result, jam is thicker and gloppier than jelly.

If the rind has been included in the jam-making process, the result is *marmalade*.

If the fruit has been slightly less pulped, it's not jam but *preserves*.

One of the appeals of desserts, jellies, and jams is their sweetness, which is the result of one of these . . .

Dextrose/Fructose/Glucose/Sucrose

Here are some short and sweet distinctions.

Glucose is a mildly sweet form of sugar, found in a number of fruits and in animal tissue.

Dextrose, also known as *corn sugar*, is a somewhat sweeter sugar obtained from starch via acid hydrolysis (decomposition).

Sucrose is the sugar obtained from sugarcane, sugar beet, and sorghum (a cereal grass). Sucrose is very sweet and is the basis of commercially manufactured sugar.

Fructose is even sweeter than sucrose, a sugar found in honey and many fruits and used as an additive in many foods.

Apple Juice/Apple Cider

Take an apple, press it, and what've you got? (Besides glucose, that is.)

You have *apple cider*, either *sweet cider* (drunk before fermentation) or *hard cider* (after fermentation)—the latter of which lives up to the word's late Latin root *sicera*, or "strong drink." *Applejack* is a brandy distilled from hard cider (making it a rather questionable name for the kiddy breakfast cereal).

For the more civilized among us, there's *apple juice*, which is cider that's been pasteurized and cleaned up for kids the world over.

Liquid/Fluid

You're at a long and boring dinner party. As you drink the beverage that was served with your meal, you find yourself wondering exactly what it is, liquid or fluid.

Turns out it's both, although a substance that's fluid isn't always a liquid.

A *liquid* is any substance that flows—that is, its molecules move freely and change shape without separating—but, unlike a gas, it does not expand indefinitely. Everything from water to blood to lava (see entry, page 129) are liquids, although chances are good you'll only see one of them at the table.

A *fluid* is any substance that flows at a steady rate, be it a liquid or a gas.

Something that's *wet* is either soaked with a liquid *or* is in a liquid state.

Club Soda/Mineral Water/Seltzer/Soda Water/ Sparkling Water/Spring Water

It used to be that when you were at a restaurant and you asked for water, the waiter knew exactly what to bring. No more. Here are the different kinds of water you can order:

Mineral water is water that contains dissolved salts and other minerals (calcium, sodium, etc.) that are good for us; it occurs naturally or it can be manufactured. Two kinds of mineral water are *hard water*, which contains a great deal of mineral matter, and *soft water*, which contains very little. Because of mineral buildup, hard water isn't good for your household pipes, although it cleans much more effectively because of the "grit" than soft water.

Heavy water, which you don't want to drink, is water in which the hydrogen (the "H" of H_2O) has been replaced by the isotope deuterium. It's the water used to slow down the neutrons produced by fission (see entry, page 39) in nuclear reactors.

Seltzer is mineral water that's been pumped full of air and thus effervesces. It's named after Selters, a town in Germany where the waters occur naturally—although there, and in markets, the "real" stuff is called *spring water* or *sparkling spring water*.

Soda water, also known as *club soda* or *sparkling water* is carbonated water that bubbles like seltzer: however, it's regular water, not mineral water, that has been pumped with carbon dioxide and is used for making ice-cream sodas, mixed drinks, etc.

Champagne/Sparkling Wine

While we're busy making bubbles, people who are celebrating invariably order champagne, although what they get may not be champagne but merely sparkling wine.

Sparkling wine is wine that becomes naturally carbonated due to a second fermentation—which, for the best taste, is ideally done in the bottle.

Champagne is sparkling wine that comes from a particular region of that name, located south of Paris. (Centuries ago, the term included any wine from this area.) Champagne is made from only the finest grapes and undergoes approximately one hundred separate steps from vine to bottle—sixty percent *more* than the cheaper, sparkling wines.

In the U.S., it is permissible—if inaccurate—for any sparkling wine to be called champagne.

Alcohol/Liqueur/Liquor/Wine

Moving to beverages not quite so festive, there's a wider variety of distinctive drinks one can order.

Alcohol is the intoxicating element in fermented beverages such as wine, beer, or spirits (see liquor, below) and is the result of the fermentation of various carbohydrates such as grain, starch, sugar, molasses, etc.

Liquor is an alcoholic beverage that is mildly distilled (purified by vaporization and condensation), such as whiskey or rum, or spirituous (strongly distilled and usually containing more alcohol), such as gin. Colloquially, the word "alcohol" is often used in place of "liquor."

Liqueur (also known as a *cordial*) is any strong, sweet, often syrupy, highly flavored spirituous drink, such as absinthe or Chartreuse. These drinks are often served as aperitifs.

Finally, of course, there's *wine*, which is the fermented juice of grapes. Wine can be white or red, sugary or not (sweet or dry), and "strengthened" with alcohol.

Ale/Beer/Lager/Stout

Despite the increased popularity wines have enjoyed in the United States over the last two decades, the most popular alcoholic beverage remains beer. And what makes beer different from similar drinks is the grain.

Beer is a mildly alcoholic beverage made from barley or some other cereal, which is malted (steeped in water, then dried in a kiln), ground, and brewed. Hops or other bitter substances are then added, and the mixture is allowed to ferment.

Lager (or *lager beer*) is aged for several months after the brewing process, and, as a result, isn't as full-bodied.

Ale is made in much the same way as beer, although it is brewed at a higher temperature and doesn't ferment as long. Because the hotter brewing process lessens the water content of ale, it usually has a greater alcoholic concentration than beer.

Stout is a strong, dark brown beer or ale, brewed hotter, and, thus, containing an even greater percentage of alcohol.

That's how they are *made*. As for what one drinks them in . . .

Cup/Mug/Stein/Tankard/Toby

Until the advent of polystyrene foam—better known by its trademarked name Styrofoam—a *cup* was any small, open vessel for beverages, and was usually bowl-shaped with a handle. The term was also used to describe such a vessel without a handle, such as that which was used for soup.

With the coming of plastic foam, the term cup came to mean any drinking vessel that's wider at the top than it is at the bottom.

Although cup means several things, receptacles in the mug family have bucked the onslaught of technology and have retained their original meanings.

A *mug* is a stone, earthenware, glass, or metal (usually copper or silver) drinking vessel, most often cylindrical and with a handle.

A *stein* is a mug with a cover and decorations, either

painted or done in bas-relief. It is usually used for serving beer.

A *tankard* is a large stein, often without the decorations, and a *toby* is a mug in the shape of a stout man wearing a tricorn hat, which forms the pouring spouts.

The reason most of these vessels are so deep is to accommodate the head that forms on beer or ale, a covering of . . .

Foam/Froth/Suds

Why is a head on beer called suds or foam but not froth? Why is the rubber called foam and not suds? It has to do with the size of the bubbles that comprise it.

Foam is a collection of very tiny bubbles that forms on the surface of a liquid due to shaking, fermentation, etc.

Froth is the same, only the bubbles are larger and more evanescent (hence, the use of the word to describe anything light or ephemeral). It would take very little pressure indeed to cause "froth rubber" to pop.

Suds are foam or froth on the surface of soapy water. The word is synonymous with beer due to their resemblance to a head of beer. (The two have often been compared in taste as well.)

Bar/Pub/Saloon/Tavern

If you were to play a game of word association, the following combinations would probably occur with some frequency: bar/neon, pub/darts, saloon/cowboys (or Matt Dillon), and tavern/inn. And although all of these places serve alcohol, they've managed to carve out very separate identities.

A *bar* is any counter (hence "bar," as in a bar of wood) where alcoholic beverages and usually light snacks are served. A place housing such a structure is a *barroom* or *bar and grill*, although "bar" itself is also often used to describe the room or building. In certain specific uses, such as snack bar, a bar is a counter where food is served with non-alcoholic beverages.

A *pub* is short for public house, and is the British term for barroom.

A *saloon* is an outgrowth of the home salon, a fancy or tacky barroom for relaxing, playing cards and/or pool, and drinking alcohol. In the American West, saloons were popular recreational spots for cowboys and were frequently part of a hotel or brothel.

A *tavern* was originally the part of an inn (see entry, page 118) where alcoholic beverages and meals were served. Today, the term applies to any barroom that serves full meals rather than just snacks.

However, people who just want to eat usually don't go to a tavern but to a . . .

Delicatessen/Luncheonette

A *delicatessen* is a store in which prepared, cooked foods are sold, with the emphasis on meats such as salami, corned beef, and pastrami, loaves of freshly baked bread, and side dishes from coleslaw to macaroni salad. Delicatessens may have a small section with self-service tables, or they may have a full restaurant area. Delicatessens tend to have an ethnic slant, especially a Jewish or Italian one. (In other words, don't go into a deli and order bologna on white bread with mayo. That's like ordering milk in Dodge City.)

A *luncheonette* is a restaurant where light meals or snacks are served at tables or at a counter, usually in conjunction with a soda fountain; it can be a stand-alone store or a section of a larger building, such as a department store. Luncheonettes traditionally specialize in hamburgers, hot dogs, and club sandwiches (two layers of sliced meat and trimmings between three slices of bread), usually served in "plates"—that is, with side orders of fries, coleslaw, and pickles.

CITIES AND TOWNS

Avenue/Boulevard/Drive/Lane/
Path/Road/Street/Trail

Here are a pair of entries that will make you a roads scholar.

A *road* is any long, narrow stretch between two points, with a smooth or paved surface for walking, biking, or traveling by motor vehicle. A *drive* is a short road.

A *path* is a narrow walkway usually defined by constant foot traffic that has trodden the surface down. A path can also be covered with stone, slate, asphalt, or the like, as a garden path. It can also form a loop, thus returning to its own beginning. A path through a largely uncharted region is called a *trail*.

A *lane* is a narrow way between high walls, hedges, fences, etc., or, in automotive terms, it's a road wide enough to accommodate just one vehicle comfortably.

A *street* is a paved public thoroughfare with a sidewalk; the term can also include the buildings adjoining it. A wide street is an *avenue* (in many major cities, avenues run perpendicular to streets), while a wide avenue is called a *boulevard*.

For people on the go, there are bigger roads to use. . . .

Expressway/Freeway/Highway/Parkway/
Route/Thruway/Turnpike

The term *highway* is the oldest term used to describe spacious, and, later, high-speed roadways. It dates back to around the twelfth century, the "high" meaning "chief," not "height." The term was used to describe the main road between any town or city.

Turnpike is the next oldest thoroughfare, a term dating back to the fourteenth century and describing a wooden pike that sat in front of a highway and wasn't raised until a toll was paid. Today, the term usually describes any three-lane highway on which a toll is paid.

A *route* is a two-to-four-lane road, which—unlike the rest of the roads in this entry—can also be used by bicycle and pedestrian traffic. Until the advent of high-speed highways toward the middle of this century, routes were one-or-two-lane roads and were the best kept public roads for travel between states and even across the country. The word first appeared in the sixteenth century, when it was used to describe the roads cut through woods by the military.

In the twentieth century, vehicular traffic has spawned the creation of new kinds of thoroughfares, all of which are variations on the highway and turnpike.

A *thruway* is a highway where access is limited; that is, to keep traffic moving quickly, vehicles can enter from intersecting streets and avenues only at well-spaced intervals. Thruways are three lanes in each direction, and tolls are often charged.

All other highways are variations of the thruway: an *expressway* is a thruway designed to accommodate four lanes of traffic, allowing for travel at relatively high speeds: a *freeway* is an expressway for which no toll is charged; and a *parkway* is a thruway on which only noncommercial traffic is permitted.

Borough/City/Community/County/ Hamlet/Town/Village

Nowadays, highways of one kind or another provide direct access to many populated areas—many, but not all. Two places that take some planning and often a 4×4 to reach are often one of these:

A *village*, a group of houses and businesses usually located in a rural area, and a *hamlet*, a very small village that usually relies on nearby hamlets or villages to provide services it lacks.

Conversely, you should have no trouble finding a modern roadway to take you to any of the following:

A *town* (or township), a large village usually located in a suburban area; and a *county*, a small administrative district comprised of several towns. In theory, this helps state officials attend more quickly to local needs, such needs being less likely to attract attention if they come from a single town.

A *city* is a large to very large town. Big cities *(aka metropolises)* are often divided into incorporated municipalities known as *boroughs*.

A *community* can be part of a town or city. Geographically, it's a vaguely defined region whose occupants usually share the same culture and heritage, and almost always the same civic interests.

Ghetto/Slum

Contrary to popular misconception, "ghetto" has not always meant a run-down section of a city.

The word comes from the Italian *borghetto*, which was coined to describe any little settlement outside the city walls (see *Fort/Fortress*, page 35). Shortened to *ghetto*, the word came to mean a section of any European city with a heavy, exclusive population of Jews. It was not a run-down area, simply a segregated one. In the United States, in the early 1800s, the word was taken to mean largely that: any area of the city largely populated by one minority group, whether it be Jews, Irish, Germans, etc.

Because city services tend to deteriorate in some minority regions due to prejudice, relative poverty, and high crime, ghettos nowadays tend to be *slums*, heavily populated, dilapidated parts of a city in which its poorest citizens dwell. Tragically, though ghetto and slum may not mean the same thing, they have certainly become one and the same.

HOME AND HEARTH

Castle/Château/Palace

Every monarch needs a place to hang his or her crown, and, naturally, that place must be fit—well, fit for a king (or queen). These abodes certainly fill the bill.

A *castle* is the fortified residence of a lord, prince, or king or queen in the Middle Ages. Depending upon the era and locale, the term also includes much or all of the town, which was built inside the castle walls for protection. A *château* is a castle in a French-speaking country.

A *palace* is the ornate official residence of a sovereign, high-ranking noble, or clergyman. Palaces were common in ancient Egypt, Greece, Asia, and the Orient, and finally in Europe in the late seventeenth century, when invasion was no longer a common threat. As a result, palaces usually were not fortified with walls but were protected by an elite palace guard.

Wigwam/Tepee

The Native Americans had many words for the tents in which they lived, but the preeminent ones are wigwam and tepee.

A *wigwam* was any kind of hut, tent, or lodge. It was usually rounded or oval in shape, formed from bark, mats, or skins laid onto poles. The word came from the Algonquin *weekuwom* ("their house").

A *tepee* was almost always a cone-shaped tent, a frame of poles fastened together where they converged at the top and covered with skins. The word was derived from the Siouan *ti* ("to dwell") and *pi* ("used for").

Another Native American home was the *hogan*—a Navaho word—which, unlike the other two, was a domed structure built entirely of branches and covered with mud or sod.

Bungalow/Hut/Lean-to

Given their interest in the mysticism of India, it was probably karma that drove the Beatles to sing about Bungalow Bill instead of Hut Harry or Lean-to Larry.

Bungalow comes from the Hindu word *banglā*, meaning "the houses of Bengal." A bungalow was originally a one-story house, thatched or tiled and usually surrounded by a veranda. Later, it came to mean any one-story dwelling.

A *hut* is a smaller dwelling, usually made of logs, grass, and sod. A Quonset hut—which is a trademarked name—is a semicylindrical metal hut used by the military for living or storage.

A *lean-to* is a shelter supported at one side by logs or trees and having an inclined roof that forms the other side.

Brick/Ceramic/Clay/Earthenware/ Porcelain/Terra-Cotta

Like logs and grasses, *clay* has always been one of the building blocks of civilization. It consists primarily of hydrated (watery) aluminum salts, and is malleable when wet, hard when dry. When exposed to the air, clay will harden; when baked in an oven or furnace (a kiln), it will become harder still, as more of its water is vaporized. At 850 degrees, brick will be tough ... but not as tough as if it's baked at 2,000 degrees or more.

Clay can be used in different ways, with functions both inside buildings and out. When used for any utilitarian purpose, clay is called *ceramic*, from the Greek *keramikos*, "potter's clay."

Brick, which was first used in 3500 B.C., is clay that has been formed into rectangular blocks and hardened by baking at extremely high temperatures. The iron content of the clay determines the strength and color of the brick; the darker it is, the stronger it is.

Earthenware is pottery made from coarse clay—that is, where the granules are larger than in regular clay.

Porcelain is a fine, vitreous (glassy), translucent clay used to make vases, statuettes, etc., that are usually covered with a transparent glaze.

Terra-cotta is clay used primarily for large statues or ornamental architecture. The sculpting is usually done before the clay has solidified.

The drawback to baking clay products of any kind is if the clay hasn't been properly and thoroughly "thrown" and kneaded, and air bubbles are trapped inside, the gas will expand when heated and cause the piece to explode, taking nearby pieces with it. That's why it might be a better idea to make things out of . . .

Cement/Concrete

Here's a distinction that isn't hard to grasp.

Cement is a blend of powdered or burned clay and limestone. When combined with sand and/or gravel and water, the mixture hardens to form *concrete*.

So the next time someone offers to fit you for a pair of cement boots, don't worry. When you hit the drink, just shake off the particles and swim for your life!

Cooperative/Condominium

You're buying a condo; your building is going co-op. What's the difference?

If you're buying a *condominium*, you're purchasing a unit in a building and sharing common areas such as the lobby and elevators.

If you're buying into a *cooperative*, the money you pay for the apartment actually buys you a share of the corporation that's been formed to own and manage the building. If you move, you aren't selling your abode, per se, but your share in the company.

In both cases, you're now your own landlord, paying an

additional fee into a pool that's used to hire doormen, groundskeepers, etc.

However, as proud as you are of your new place in the city, you like to get away from the hustle and rush once in a while, so you also buy a home in the country, where you can sit outside a spell and relax on one of these. . . .

Deck/Patio/Porch/Portico/Stoop/Veranda

You're sitting on a swing chair, the scent of jasmine in your nostrils, an iced tea in your hand, when suddenly it occurs to you: You have no idea what kind of structure this is, this place where you spend so many of your leisure hours.

Look around you. If it's an uncovered area, usually paved, attached to the house, and serving as an area for outdoor living, it's a *patio*. It's a *deck* if it's a wooden variation of the above, and a *stoop* if it's a small deck.

If it's an outdoor addition to a building, a covered area or large vestibule beside a doorway, it's a *porch*. If it's a porch that's only partly enclosed, it's a *veranda*.

If it's a smaller structure beside a doorway, with a roof that's usually supported by columns, it's a *portico*.

As you look around, you notice a few loose shingles and decide to get a hammer and nails to secure them. You head inside, go down the stairs, and realize you don't know whether you're heading into the . . .

Basement/Cellar

Since a basement and a cellar are two different things, does that mean a sports team can't be in both at the same time?

Sportswriters—relax. They sure can.

A *basement* is a story just below the main floor, and either wholly or partly underground. The only story that can possibly be any lower is the subbasement.

A *cellar* is a room or group of rooms located in the basement. Cellars usually describe an area used for storing things, such as food, wine, coal, Yankees, etc.

So a sports team can be in two places at once—and in three, if you count the doghouse . . . where many fans put a losing team.

Chamber/Room

Now your mind's racing. You know about your house outside and downstairs, but what about the main living area? Is it full of rooms or chambers?

A *room* is any interior space in a house or apartment that is enclosed by walls or partitions. In a public place or place of business, a room is called an office, from the Latin *officium*, "a duty." A very small office is a *cubicle*.

A *chamber* is a personal room in a house designed to provide privacy, such as a bedroom or bathroom. It's where people do things that are inappropriate for other rooms of the house. In a public place or place of business, a chamber is also a private room, such as a judge's chambers, where professionals conduct business or hold meetings.

Looking Glass/Mirror

In 1871, Alice went *Through the Looking Glass*. At the time, readers knew just what author Lewis Carroll meant. Today, however, many people assume the title refers to a mirror of a particular size, which it doesn't.

A *mirror* is any polished substance that reflects rays of light, thus re-creating the image exactly, albeit in reverse. Ancient civilizations made mirrors out of highly polished metal.

A *looking glass* is a specific kind of mirror, one made of glass and coated on the back with quicksilver or a similar reflective amalgam. The term was coined to differentiate the high quality of the coated glass from a polished metal surface.

It would have been tough for Alice to squeeze through a hand-held looking glass, but that's why Carroll had artist John Tenniel working with him: to show readers just what kind of a looking glass he had in mind!

Bedspread/Blanket/Cover/Coverlet/Quilt

Very few of us like to make the bed when we get up, especially when there are several layers to make. Whatever the layer, any fabric that goes over you when you sleep is a *cover*. There are two kinds of covers:

A *blanket*, which is usually made of soft woolen cloth and isn't very heavy; and a *quilt*, which is made from two layers of cloth filled with down or a soft fabric and stitched together in patterns.

After you wake up, one of the following is usually spread on top of the bed:

A *bedspread*, which is a decorative outer covering, or a *coverlet*, an ornamental quilt that is spread over a blanket or quilt. The latter can also be used as blankets on very cold nights . . . or if you don't feel like unmaking the bed when you go to sleep.

Couch/Sofa

At least as far back as the fourteenth century, a *couch* was any kind of long frame supporting a cushion and used for sleeping. (Remember cooing to a member of the opposite sex, "Voulez-vous coucher avec moi?" Your intention was definitely *not* to sit down.) Today, a couch is still something on which you're supposed to recline.

In Eastern countries, some four centuries ago, a *sofa* was simply a section of the floor that was raised a foot or so, either by a built-in platform or a movable framework, and covered with sumptuous rugs and cushions. The Europeans modified the concept, transforming sofas into long seats with cushions, a back, and sides, and used to seat several people at once. Folks who recline on a sofa are considered rude. For sleeping, you use a sofa bed . . . or a couch.

While we're on the subject, a *settee* is a form of sofa, often armless and usually for two people; a *divan* is another form of sofa, almost always without a back or arms and nestled against a wall; a *chesterfield* is a couch with thick seats, and arms as high as the high back; and a *meridienne* is a sofa having sides of different height connected by a sloping back.

Cord/Rope/String/Thread/Twine

A ragged length of rope, tied in a sheepshank, hailed a cab.

"Say," said the startled driver, "aren't you a rope?"

"No," said the passenger. "I'm a frayed knot."

Would the joke have worked with twine or cord? Knot really, because there isn't much to be frayed on either of them.

Thread is the thinnest unit of line, made of a strand or twisted strands of spun silk, cotton, flax, etc.

Twine is two or three strands of thread twisted together; *string* is a thin line of interwoven fibers or four or more twisted threads.

Cord is a thick string, made up of several strands twisted together, while *rope* is thicker still, made from intertwined strands of cord or wire, leather strips, fiber, etc.

Now that we've laid thread bare, what can you do with it? . . .

Sew/Stitch/Suture

If you put a threaded needle through material in such a way as to create a single loop, what you've done is *stitch*, made a single in-and-out movement with the needle. Several stitches in succession can be used to make repairs or create designs.

When you use stitches to join two pieces of fabric or to repair material, you are *sewing*.

Needlework or embroidery is stitching, but it's not sewing. Repairing a wound is stitching, though the correct term is *suturing*, from the Latin *suĕre*, "to sew."

Sew there!

Coat/Jacket

There's a very good reason your tongue can be coated but not jacketed: only by coating it can you cover it completely. On the other hand, if there were such a thing as a book coat instead of a book jacket, you'd have much more covering than you'd need.

A *coat* is an outer garment with sleeves, covering at least the upper part of the body and usually more.

A *jacket* is a sleeved coat that reaches no lower than the waist and is often worn with the front open.

Since we're already covering outerwear (a redundancy?), a *sport jacket* is cut somewhat fuller than the jacket of a business suit and is usually made of patterned fabric; a *blazer* is a solid-colored sport jacket, usually with metal buttons and frequently with an insignia on the breast pocket.

A *dinner jacket* is a formal, tailless jacket with satin lapels (*aka* a *tuxedo*, named after a country club in Tuxedo Park, New York), and a *swallowtail coat* is a full-dress coat that tapers into two long tails in the back.

However, if you're going out and want to be really formal, try one of these on for size....

Cape/Cloak

Think Dracula. Think Batman.

Two figures who define the word "mysterious" largely because they wear a *cape*, a sleeveless garment fastened around the neck and falling from the shoulders. Capes are typically black for men (sometimes lined with silk, often red) and white for women.

A *cloak* is a somewhat fuller, less dashing outer garment fastened at the neck and also without sleeves. Because it's worn over the clothing during cold or inclement weather, cloaks are usually made of heavier material than capes, have buttons in the front to secure them, and frequently sport a hood (*aka* a *cowl*), especially women's cloaks.

A cloak is preferable to a coat because it doesn't cause a jacket worn underneath it to bunch.

Detergent/Soap

You clean your body with soap and your clothes with detergent. Does that mean if there's no soap handy, you can scrub down with Tide or Ecover?

No reason you can't. Whether liquid, powdered, caked, or flaked, a soap or detergent is any cleaning agent that holds on to insoluble matter and carries it away. Both soap and detergent molecules have an end that's attracted to water, the other to oily dirt, grease, or bacteria. The difference is all in what they're made of and how well they hold grime.

Soap comes from animal or vegetable fat or oils, such as olive oil.

Detergent (and the chemically similar *shampoo*) was invented early in this century, derived primarily from petroleum, coal tar, and similar substances. Because of their more complex chemical makeup, detergents: (a) work harder to get dirt out [they have to; you don't scrub them in]; and (b) hold on to dirt tighter, so it won't settle back in. Detergents are also designed not to mix with salt in the water, which keeps the wash from getting "scummy."

So why use soap at all? Because it's cheaper and works fine for small scrubbing jobs at hand—so to speak.

Epithet/Moniker/Nickname/Sobriquet/Surname

That which we call a rose by any other name would smell as sweet, though not if it's a surname: you wouldn't want to go around calling Pete Rose sweet!

A *surname* is a person's last name, his or her family name as opposed to a first name (*aka* a given or Christian name).

An *epithet* is any word or phrase that replaces or is added to a person's name to describe them or a characteristic attribute, such as Peter the Great or Wilt the Stilt.

Technically, a *moniker* is a person's full name, although the word is often used synonymously with a *nickname*, an informal name used in place of a person's proper name and inspired by their habits, attributes, appearance, etc., such as

Scarface for Al Capone or the Yankee Clipper for Joe DiMaggio.

A *sobriquet* is an assumed name, although the term is usually used to describe a stage name, such as Adam West for Bill Anderson. (On the other hand, Marion Michael Morrison changed his name legally to John Wayne, so it wasn't a sobriquet. The Duke, of course, was a nickname.)

First Cousin/First Cousin Once Removed/ Second Cousin

To Shakespeare, a cousin was any kinsman or kinswoman.

But no more. A cousin is a specific relative, beginning with the *first cousin*, the offspring of your aunt and/or uncle, also known as a *full cousin*.

As the apples fall further from the tree, the relationships (and terms) get a bit more complicated.

To you, a *second cousin* is the child of a parent's first cousin, but a *first cousin once removed* can be two things: either your first cousin's child, or, less commonly, the first cousin of your parent.

Etiquette (and most parents) demand that first cousins once removed be invited to big family bashes, whereas second cousins generally aren't considered close enough to matter. (Until they're not invited—and then, as Einstein once observed, "Everything is relative.")

SELECTED
BIBLIOGRAPHY

The ABC's of Nature. Richard L. Scheffel, editor. Pleasantville, New York: Reader's Digest Association, 1984.

Amo, Amas, Amat and More. Eugene Ehrlich. New York: Harper & Row, 1985.

Birds. Herbert S. Zim and Ira N. Gabrielson. New York: Western Publishing Co., 1956.

The Book of Answers. Barbara Berliner with Melinda Corey and George Ochoa. New York: Prentice Hall Press, 1990.

The Book of Jargon. Don Ethan Miller. New York: Collier Books, 1981.

The Cambridge Encyclopedia of Language. David Crystal. New York: Press Syndicate of the University of Cambridge, 1987.

The Concise Dictionary of 26 Languages. Peter M. Bergman, editor. New York: New American Library, 1968.

Descriptionary. Marc McCutcheon. New York: Ballantine Books, 1993.

Dictionary of American Slang. Harold Wentworth and Stuart Berg Flexner, editors. New York: Thomas Y. Crowell, 1975.

Dictionary of Science. Siegfried Mandel. New York: Dell Publishing, 1975.

The Encyclopedia of How It Works. Donald Clarke, editor. New York: A & W Publishers, 1977.

The Encyclopedia of Mammals. Dr. David Macdonald, editor. New York: Facts on File Publications, 1984.

An Exaltation of Larks. James Lipton. New York: Viking Penguin, 1991.

The Facts on File Dictionary of Science. E. B. Uvarov and Alan Isaacs. New York: Facts on File Publications, 1986.

Famous First Facts. Joseph Nathan Kane. New York: Ace Books, 1974.

An Incomplete Education. Judy Jones and William Wilson. New York: Ballantine Books, 1987.

Insects of the World. Jeanne E. Remington. New York: Bantam Books, 1975.

Isaac Asimov's Guide to Earth and Space. Isaac Asimov. New York: Random House, 1991.

The Joy of Mathematics. Theoni Pappas. San Carlos, California: Wide World Publishing, 1989.

The New Book of Knowledge. William E. Shapiro, editor. Danbury, Connecticut: Grolier International, 1980.

The New College Encyclopedia of Music. J. A. Westrup and F. L. Harrison. New York: W.W. Norton and Co., 1976.

The New York Public Library Desk Reference. New York: The New York Public Library and Stonesong Press, 1989.

The Oxford English Dictionary. London: Oxford University Press, 1971.

Phrase and Word Origins. Alfred H. Holt. New York: Dover Publications, 1961.

Putnam's Contemporary French Dictionary. Gustave Rudler and Norman C. Anderson. New York: Berkley Publishing Group, 1974.

Putnam's Contemporary Italian Dictionary. Isopel May. New York: Berkley Publishing Group, 1977.

Putnam's Contemporary Spanish Dictionary. R. F. Brown. New York: Berkley Publishing Group, 1977.

Reader's Digest Book of Facts. Pleasantville, New York: Reader's Digest Association, 1987.

The Reader's Encyclopedia. William Rose Benet. New York: Thomas Y. Crowell, 1965.

Webster's New Universal Unabridged Dictionary. Jean L. McKechnie, editor. New York: Simon & Schuster, 1983.

What's What. Reginald Bragonier, Jr., and David Fisher. New York: Ballantine Books, 1981.

Why Do We Say It? Book Sales. New York: Castle Publishing, 1985.

The World Almanac and Book of Facts. Mark S. Hoffman, editor. New York: Pharos Books, 1992.